Europeans and their rights

Freedom of religion

in European constitutional and
international case law

Renáta Uitz
Associate professor of comparative constitutional law
Central European University,
Budapest

Council of Europe Publishing

French version:
La liberté de religion
ISBN 978-92-871-6204-5

The opinions expressed in this work are the responsibility of the author and do not necessarily reflect the official policy of the Council of Europe.

All rights reserved. No part of this publication may be translated, reproduced or transmitted, in any form or by any means, electronic (CD-Rom, Internet, etc.) or mechanical, including photocopying, recording or any information storage or retrieval system, without prior permission in writing from the Public Information and Publications Division, Directorate of Communication (F-67075 Strasbourg Cedex or publishing@coe.int).

Cover design: Graphic Design Studio, Council of Europe
Layout: Editions européennes

Council of Europe Publishing
F-67075 Strasbourg Cedex
http://book.coe.int

ISBN 978-92-871-6201-4
© Council of Europe, August 2007
Printed in Belgium

"Europeans and their rights" series

Are there common European rights? This series of publications aims to answer this question through a comparative study of the protection given by constitutions and conventions to the civil and political rights guaranteed by the European Convention on Human Rights.

Each volume studies a specific individual right based on practical examples and relevant decisions by European constitutional courts or the European Court of Human Rights.

The series uses information obtained from the Codices database, an electronic publication by the European Commission for Democracy through Law (usually called the Venice Commission). The Codices database (www.codices.coe.int) contains periodic reports of the case law of the constitutional courts of the 47 Council of Europe member states and courts of equivalent jurisdiction in Europe, including the European Court of Human Rights (Council of Europe) and the Court of Justice of the European Communities (European Union).

In both the Codices database and this series of publications, decisions are presented in the following way:

1. *Identification*
    - a) *country or organisation*
    - b) *name of the court*
    - c) *chamber or division (if any)*
    - d) *date of the decision*
    - e) *number of the decision or case*
    - f) *title (if any)*
    - g) *official publication*
    - h) *non-official publications*

Contents

Chapter 1 – Introduction: Protection of freedom of religion or belief in European democracies 9

1.1. Freedom of religion in international documents and national constitutions in Europe: An overview 10

1.2. Secularity, tolerance and pluralism in European democracies 15

Chapter 2 – Freedom of religion as an individual right 23

2.1. What amounts to religion or protected belief? 24

2.2. The scope of *forum internum* and protected manifestations of freedom of religion 29

Interference with the forum internum?
Revealing convictions: registration of religious affiliation 34

Refusing to take an oath: A decision within the forum internum *or a proper manifestation of religious freedom?* 38

Religious holiday, Sunday laws and faith-based days of rest 42

	Manifestations of religious freedom: facially neutral limitations and the problem of ritual slaughter	49
	Manifestations of religious freedom: refusing blood transfusion on grounds of conscience	53
2.3.	Proselytism	55
2.4.	Conscientious objection to military service	66

Chapter 3 – Rights of religious communities and associations 85

3.1.	The basis of church–state relations: Registering religious associations	87
	Fundamental premises of religious association law	91
	An overview of problems with conditions applicable to recognising religious organisations	94
	Registration as a precondition of collective religious exercise	97
	Proving social acceptance: membership criteria	100
	Mandatory waiting periods	102
	Further limitations of religious freedom stemming from legal definitions in regulations on religious association	104
	Church autonomy: The role of religious perspectives in registration processes	105
3.2.	Education and religious instruction	109
	Introduction: parental rights and state duties	112
	Denominational private schools	115
	Religious education in public schools	117
	Control over the educational environment and the prohibition of indoctrination	119
	The right to be exempted from religious activities	122

Religious symbols in school:
The limits of religious tolerance and pluralism 124

3.3. **Accommodation in prisons
and military establishments** 132

*Basic theoretical and practical problems with
accommodation in restricted environments* 135

*Limitations of religious freedom
in prisons and the military* 140

*Prohibition of taking advantage
of a restricted environment* 144

Chapter 4 – Contemporary problems and challenges 147

4.1. **The prohibition of blasphemy: Between freedom
of expression and religious freedom** 148

4.2. **On the governmental obligation
to protect against dangerous religions** 164

*New religious movements
and the label of brainwashing* 167

Enquete commissions and sect observatories 170

Select bibliography and suggested further reading 179

Chapter 1
Introduction: Protection of freedom of religion or belief in European democracies

The aim of the present work is to provide an overview of European human rights and constitutional jurisprudence on religious freedom. Decisions of national courts and the European Court of Human Rights (ECtHR) were selected on issues and problems which appear to (re)surface across Europe time and time again. Extensive excerpts from judicial decisions form the backbone of the work.[1] Commentaries add details from national contexts which assist in discovering the roots of similarities and differences in judicial stances on religious freedom issues. The limitations of this endeavour are clear from the outset and need to be acknowledged at the start. On the one hand, in such a brief comparative analysis of constitutional jurisprudence the space for a critical review of pertinent literature is scarce. On the other hand, a comparative analysis allows for the exposition of a select set of problems in numerous jurisdictions at the expense of leaving other, equally significant matters behind. For instance the chapter on church–state relations covers religious instruction in public education, while it does not deal with state funding for religious organisations. Due to spatial limitations, several similar strategic decisions had to be taken which in no way intend to question the practical or jurisprudential significance of issues and problems that are not covered in the following pages.

---

1. Summaries of constitutional court decisions are cited from the Codices database maintained by the Venice Commission. The manuscript was closed on 31 December 2006. This is also the date when websites were last visited.

Before turning to a discussion of jurisprudence, Chapter 1 has a short introduction which glances at fundamental concepts associated with the protection of religious freedom in international instruments and national constitutions across Europe. Thereafter, in Chapter 2, individual religious freedom is discussed, with special attention to proselytism and conscientious objection to military service. Chapter 3 is devoted to church–state relations, focusing on problems in the recognition of religious associations, religious instruction in public schools and religious freedom in the armed forces and detention facilities. Lastly, Chapter 4 covers such contemporary problems and challenges as the prohibition of blasphemy and the duty of the state to collect and provide information on new religious movements.[2]

1.1. Freedom of religion in international documents and national constitutions in Europe: An overview

Freedom of religion or belief is protected by numerous international instruments. The Universal Declaration of Human Rights, Article 18,[3] proclaims that:

> Everyone has the right to freedom of thought, conscience and religion; this right includes freedom to change his religion or belief, and freedom, either alone or in community with others and in public or private, to manifest his religion or belief in teaching, practice, worship and observance.

In a much more detailed fashion, Article 18 of the International Covenant on Civil and Political Rights (ICCPR)[4] provides that:

> 1. Everyone shall have the right to freedom of thought, conscience and religion. This right shall include freedom to have or to adopt a religion or belief of his choice, and freedom, either individually or in community with others and in public

---

2. Note that a separate chapter was not devoted to religious discrimination; instead, pertinent problems are discussed in the context of particular constitutional problems.
3. Adopted and proclaimed by General Assembly Resolution 217A (III) of 10 December 1948.
4. Adopted and opened for signature, ratification and accession by General Assembly Resolution 2200A (XXI) of 16 December 1966.

or private, to manifest his religion or belief in worship, observance, practice and teaching.

2. No one shall be subject to coercion which would impair his freedom to have or to adopt a religion or belief of his choice.

3. Freedom to manifest one's religion or beliefs may be subject only to such limitations as are prescribed by law and are necessary to protect public safety, order, health, or morals or the fundamental rights and freedoms of others.

4. The States Parties to the present Covenant undertake to have respect for the liberty of parents and, when applicable, legal guardians to ensure the religious and moral education of their children in conformity with their own convictions.

The regional human rights instrument having special significance in Europe, the Convention for the Protection of Human Rights and Fundamental Freedoms provides in its Article 9 as follows:

1. Everyone has the right to freedom of thought, conscience and religion; this right includes freedom to change his religion or belief, and freedom, either alone or in community with others and in public or private, to manifest his religion or belief, in worship, teaching, practice and observance.

2. Freedom to manifest one's religion or beliefs shall be subject only to such limitations as are prescribed by law and are necessary in a democratic society in the interests of public safety, for the protection of public order, health or morals, or the protection of the rights and freedoms of others.

When comparing the language of these international instruments, it is apparent that clauses devoted to protecting religious freedom reach to encompass secular beliefs. In order to fully grasp the extent of protection meant to be offered to freedom of conscience in Article 18 of the ICCPR, it is worth consulting General Comment No. 22[5] which clarifies (at para 2) that:

Article 18 protects theistic, non-theistic and atheistic beliefs, as well as the right not to profess any religion or belief. The terms

---

5. *General Comment No. 22*: "The right to freedom of thought, conscience and religion" (Article 18), 30/07/93. CCPR/C/21/Rev.1/Add. (1993).

"belief" and "religion" are to be broadly construed. Article 18 is not limited in its application to traditional religions or to religions and beliefs with institutional characteristics or practices analogous to those of traditional religions.

The same applies to Article 9 of the ECHR and most European constitutions. In addition, a number of post-communist constitutions expressly provide for a constitutional right not to hold a belief.[6] When a constitution provides expressly for the protection of religious convictions without mentioning secular beliefs, a constitutional court may still expand the scope of constitutional protection to the latter, as evidenced by the jurisprudence of the Italian Constitutional Court.[7] Nonetheless, as Malcolm Evans pointed out – as a matter of practice – secular beliefs are more likely to be protected by Strasbourg institutions if they fall within a well-established or better-known school of thought.[8] While the present work is devoted primarily to the protection of religious freedom, it will make mention of problems concerning the protection of secular beliefs, where appropriate.

International instruments as well as national constitutions often expressly mention various aspects of religious freedom which are meant to be protected. The language of rights provisions usually distinguishes between the freedom to hold, choose and change beliefs, and the freedom to manifest thereof. Unlike in the case of other civil rights and political rights, these provisions emphasise the individual as well as the collective aspect of the right. In Europe, the positive side of religious freedom together with the intricacies of church–state relationships give rise to a complex relationship of freedom of religion as an individual right and as a right exercised in a community with others.

---

6. See, for example, Azerbaijani Constitution, Article 48.2, Belarus Constitution, Article 31, Bulgarian Constitution, Article 37.1, Czech Constitution, Article 15.1, Slovak Constitution, Article 24.1 and Ukrainian Constitution, Article 35.1.
7. See Article 19 of the Italian Constitution and ITA-1995-2-008 a) Italy; b) Constitutional Court / c) / d) 04-05-1995 / e) 149/1995 / f) / g) *Gazzetta Ufficiale*, "Prima Serie Speciale" (Official Gazette), 19, 10.05.1995 / h) Codices (Italian).
8. Evans, M. D., *Religious liberty and international law in Europe*, Cambridge, 1997, p. 291.

For most Europeans, the collective exercise of religious freedom is typically expected to take place under the auspices of a church. In states with an established state church and in states with a dominant or prevailing religious tradition, the term 'church' refers to the institutions of a particular religion. In other countries, the term is used in a more flexible sense, often without regard to whether or not national legislation refers to "churches", "religious organisations", "religious associations" and the like (e.g. "congregations") for the purposes of legal regulation. Unless specified otherwise, the following text will use these phrases interchangeably and without reference to fine distinctions in any particular national legal system.[9] (Such differences specific to a legal system will be pointed out in order to elucidate the difference in treatment attached to the differences in terminology.)

Such terms, even when used without further precision, tend to denote religious communities that are legitimate, i.e. enjoy the state's recognition, support or at least tolerance. In contrast, analysts of national exchanges, policies, legislation and jurisprudence all too often counter reference to sects and cults. As Silvio Ferrari reminds us, in many European languages the word "sect" in its origins "indicates a group of dissenters who separated from a larger religious group" and in most languages tends to have a negative (if not derogatory or denigrating) connotation.[10] The phrase "new religious movements" is often used in scholarly works to refer to the creeds which some prefer to associate with sects,[11] nonetheless, this phrase is not entirely appropriate as some of these creeds are new only in Europe and are quite ancient in their place of origin. In the following pages, the word "sect" or "cult" will be used if it is essential for canvassing the legal regulation in a particular state, while – despite the point duly made also by Ferrari – the phrase "new religious movement" will be used in all other cases where

---

9. Such nuances would be impossible to preserve due to distortions in the course of translation. Also, as a consequence of the limitations of this endeavour, the following section cannot provide a detailed overview of church registration systems in Council of Europe member states.
10. Ferrari, S., "New Religious Movements in Western Europe", *Research and Analyses*, No. 9, October 2006, available at http://religion.info/pdf/2006_10_ferrari_nrm.pdf, pp. 2-3 (internal quotations omitted).
11. See Colliard, C.-A. and Letteron, R., *Libertés publiques*, Dalloz, 2005, p. 441.

relevant and unavoidable. Nonetheless, regardless of the nuances of terminology, the very act of exclusion of communities of believers from the scope of legal protection via labelling them as a "sect", "cult", "non-traditional/new church" or the like appears as a *prima facie* undue limitation of religious freedom.[12]

In addition to protecting religious freedom and its manifestations in express terms, international instruments especially prohibit discrimination on grounds of religion. The Universal Declaration on Human Rights guarantees all the rights provided therein without grounds of religion (Article 2, also Article 25) and expressly prohibits discrimination on religious grounds (Article 26), and especially prohibits discrimination on grounds of religion in enjoying the right to marry and to found a family (Article 16(2)). The ICCPR also requires states to provide equal treatment in the enjoyment of the rights to all, irrespective of their religion (Article 2(1)), prohibits discrimination on grounds of religion also at times of emergency (Article 4(1)) and proclaims the rights of children without discrimination on grounds of religion (Article 24(1)). In addition to prohibiting various forms of discrimination on grounds of religion, the ICCPR declares protection for the rights of religious minorities (Article 27).[13] The ECHR also prohibits discrimination on the basis of religion in express terms (Article 14).[14]

The protection of religious freedom in national and international instruments is informed by the basic premise that coercion in matters of faiths or belief is unacceptable and impermissible. These prohibitions are formulated in some constitutions as a safeguard against being forced to participate in religious ceremonies,[15] while

---

12. Section 4.2 is devoted to a discussion on vigilance about what is usually called sectarian or cult activities.
13. See also Article 2 of the 1981 Declaration on the Elimination of Intolerance and Discrimination Based on Religion or Belief, proclaimed by General Assembly Resolution 36/55 of 25 November 1981.
14. Since religious discrimination is a prevalent problem which may be traced behind most cases involving a violation of religious freedom, instead of devoting a separate section to it, the following chapters integrate a discussion of discrimination issues.
15. See, for example, Albanian Constitution (Article 24.3), Austrian Constitution (1867) (Article 14.3), Finnish Constitution (Article 11.2), Lithuanian Constitution (Article 26.3), Polish Constitution (Article 53.6), Swedish Constitution (Article 2), Swiss Constitution (Article 15.3) and Turkish Constitution (Article 24.3).

other constitutions proclaim that nobody may be forced to disclose their religious affiliation.[16] General Comment No. 22 describes coercion in matters of faith as an act "that would impair the right to have or adopt a religion or belief, including the use of threat of physical force or penal sanctions to compel believers or non-believers to adhere to their religious beliefs and congregations, to recant their religion or belief or to convert."[17] In *R. v. Big M Drug Mart Ltd*, its leading decision on religious freedom, the Canadian Supreme Court described its understanding of coercion in the context of religious freedom in more comprehensive terms, saying that

> Freedom can primarily be characterised by the absence of coercion or constraint. If a person is compelled by the state or the will of another to a course of action or inaction which he would not otherwise have chosen, he is not acting of his own volition and he cannot be said to be truly free … Coercion includes not only such blatant forms of compulsion as direct commands to act or refrain from acting on pain of sanction, coercion includes indirect forms of control which determine or limit alternative courses of conduct available to others.[18]

1.2. Secularity, tolerance and pluralism in European democracies

The constitutional protection of religious freedom and freedom of conscience, thought or belief shall be seen not in isolation, but in its broader context. Any analysis of religious freedom must consider the relationship between religious freedom as just one, although rather important, aspect of liberty, individual autonomy or human dignity. The constitutional significance of protecting religious freedom is only acknowledged if the significance of freedom of religion is understood in a plural, democratic society.

When analysing European state–church relations, it is striking that in those European countries that do not house a state church or

---

16. See, for example, Azerbaijani Constitution (Article 71.4), Polish Constitution (Article 53.7), Russian Constitution (Article 29.3), Slovenian Constitution (Article 41.2), Spanish Constitution (Article 16.2) and Swedish Constitution (Article 2).
17. *General Comment No. 22*, p. 5.
18. In *R. v. Big M Drug Mart Ltd* [1985] 1 SCR 295, paragraph 95.

state religion, the relationship of the state and churches is characterised not by an uncompromising separation of church and state, but by their intensive interaction, whether this relationship is termed as co-ordination, co-operation or interdependence.[19] Interestingly, the word "separation" does not frequently appear in post-communist constitutions either. As Wojciech Sadurski reminds us, although this terminology is often rejected with reference to its negative connotations, in reality this phenomenon is better explained with the influence of dominant churches and their political allies.[20] In practice, constitutional clauses prescribing separation of church and state typically do not prevent European governments from entering into concordats or agreements of co-operation with religious organisations of their choice.

The relationship of religious associations with the state and religious freedom have been explored with great interest by academics. In Cole Durham's observations, it should not be taken for granted that from more separation of church and state, more religious liberty results: religious freedom may be achieved not only in separation-based regimes, but also in systems with an established or endorsed church, or accepting co-operation or accommodation of churches.[21] Malcolm Evans submits that "there is no need for a rigid separation of church and state provided that the state also facilitates participation of other belief communities within the broader legal and political community in a fashion which enables them to enjoy the freedom of religion."[22] The role of the state as a benefactor of religious freedom is most elegantly explained with reference to the positive aspect of fundamental rights, an obligation imposed (or claimed to be imposed) on most European governments in their

---

19. For example, the preamble of the Albanian Constitution invokes the spirit of religious coexistence and tolerance, while Article 3 names religious co-existence as a basis of the state.
20. Sadurski, W., *Rights Before Courts, A Study of Constitutional Courts in Postcommunist States of Central and Eastern Europe*, Springer, 2005, p. 136.
21. Durham, W. C., Jr., "Perspectives on Religious Liberty, A Comparative Framework", pp. 1-44, in van der Vyver, J. and Witte, J., Jr., eds, *Religious Human Rights in Global Perspective, Legal Perspectives*, Martinus Nijhoff, 1996, pp. 19 *et seq*.
22. Evans, M. D.,"Believing in Communities, European Style", pp. 133-155, in Ghanea, N., ed., *The Challenge of Religious Discrimination at the Dawn of the New Millenium*, Martinus Nijhoff, 2004, p. 149.

constitutions. As Donald Kommers summarises, "freedom of religion in the positive sense implies an obligation on the part of the state to create a social order in which it is possible for the religious personality to develop and flourish conveniently and easily."[23]

In their behaviour in matters of faith and in their actions towards religious communities, European states are guided by considerations of neutrality, secularity or *laïcité*. Within the limitations of the present work it is impossible to accord due treatment to these conceptions. It should be pointed out nonetheless that, although they refer to state–church relations, these terms are deeply imbedded in national constitutional traditions, wherein they retain numerous competing readings and they ultimately allow for so distinct practices as to make them hardly interchangeable.

For instance, Article 1 of the French Constitution proclaims that "France shall be an indivisible, secular (*laïque*), democratic and social Republic," a constitutional provision which announces the constitutional principle of *laïcité* as acknowledged by the French Constitutional Council[24] and also by the Council of State.[25] Speaking of *laïcité*, Michel Troper notes that it is a highly ambiguous term, which at its core refers to separation of church and state.[26] This separation was brought by the 1905 law on separation of church and state.[27] *Laïcité* is best understood not as a type of

---

23. Kommers, D. P., *Constitutional Jurisprudence in the Federal Republic of Germany*, Duke, 1997, second edition, p. 461.
24. FRA-1994-1-001 a) France / b) Constitutional Council / c) / d) 13-01-1994 / e) 93-329 DC / f) Law on the conditions governing investment aid for private schools granted by local authorities / g) Recueil des décisions *du Conseil constitutionnel* (Official Digest), 1994, 9 / h) Codices (French).
25. CE, *Syndicat national des enseignements du second degré*, 6 avril 2001.
26. Troper, M., "French Secularism, or Laïcité", 21, *Cardozo Law Review*, 2000, p. 1267; Gunn, T. J., "Under God but Not the Scarf: The Founding Myths of Religious Freedom in the United States and Laïcité in France", 7, *Journal of Church and State*, 2004, pp. 8-9.
On terminological difficulties and the many meanings of *laïcité* see also Bedouelle, G. and Costa, J. P., *Les laïcités à la française*, PUF, 1998.
27. This law does not apply in Alsace-Lorraine, which at the time was part of the German Empire. For an English-language summary of the French legal regulation see, for example, Garay, A. et al., "The Permissible Scope of Legal Limitations on the Freedom of Religion or Belief in France", 19, *Emory International Law Review*, 785, 2005, pp. 792-797.

church–state relationship, but as a type of state policy towards religions which does not prevent the state from endorsing religious values.[28] This explains how it is possible for the French concept of *laïcité* – which is commonly remarked to be among the most rigid separationist approaches in Europe – to allow for state ownership of religious buildings or state support for religious private schools. At the same time, *laïcité*'s tradition was noted to feed "a very strong mistrust of any religion, which becomes all the stronger the more a religion differentiates from the most known religion, i.e. Catholicism."[29]

The 1978 Spanish constitution also acknowledges separation of church and state (Article 16.3), a true innovation in Spanish constitutionalism.[30] Spanish church–state relations are governed by the four informing principles (*principios informadores*) of religious freedom, equality, neutrality, and co-operation. In the words of Javier Martínez-Torrón

> (neutrality) does not mean that civil authorities declare themselves indifferent towards the results of freedom of religion or belief, or that they withdraw completely from the content of personal choices in this particular area of human rationality ... Neutrality means that when the State acts with respect to diverse religions, it may take into account only the social effects of the religious activity, including the cases in which those effects conflict with values that the legal order considers necessary.[31]

According to the Spanish Constitutional Court the active participation of the military in a Catholic parade does not violate state neutrality (Decision ESP-1996-R-001 a) Spain / b) Constitutional Court / c) Second Chamber / d) 11-11-1996 / e) 177/1996 / f) / g) Boletín oficial del Estado (Official Gazette), 303, 17.12.1996 / h)).

---

28. Troper, *French Secularism*, p. 1271.
29. Garay, et al., *Freedom of Religion or Belief in France*, pp. 819-820.
30. Suoto Paz, J. A., "Perspectives on Religious Freedom in Spain", 2001 *Brigham Young University Law Review*, 669, 2001, p. 675. For the drafting history see idem, pp. 689 et seq.
31. Martínez-Torrón, J., "Freedom of Religion in the Case Law of the Spanish Constitutional Court", 2001, *Brigham Young University Law Review*, 711 (2001), pp. 719-720.

Indeed, secularity in Italian constitutional jurisprudence means non-confessionality of the state. As the Italian Constitutional Court puts it:

> the state cannot prescribe practices of a religious nature for either believers or non-believers, because religion belongs to a sphere which is not that of the state, whose sole function in the matter is to ensure favourable conditions for the expression of all people's freedom and, in that context, of religious freedom.
>
> Because of the distinction between the "civil" and "religious" spheres which characterises the basic constitutional principle of the state's secularity or "non-denominational attitude", the state is forbidden to enforce its precepts by invoking obligations of a religious kind. In other words, religion and the attendant moral obligations cannot be imposed as a means of furthering the ends of the state (Decision ITA-1996-R-001 a) Italy / b) Constitutional Court / c) / d) 30-09-1996 / e) 334/1996 / f) / g) *Gazzetta Ufficiale, Prima Serie Speciale* (Official Gazette), 42, 16.10.1996 / h)).

This conception of the separation of the civil and secular sphere is truly reminiscent of an understanding of secularism which originates in Latin Christian scholarship. Using Saint Thomas Aquinas as an example, John Finnis demonstrates the powers of the Church, and also the social process which delineates the sphere of the secular as a result.[32]

In an account of church and state relations in Germany, Gerhard Robbers warns that Germany is a religiously neutral state, while secularism or secularity in German has negative connotations.[33] In the words of Martin Heckel, in Germany, "the legal orders of church and state are not dependent on each other, but are basically self-coherent ... (The state is) obliged to adhere to the principles of non-identification, of neutrality in religious and ideological matters, and of parity. ... (W)hereas the state is strictly banned

---

32. Finnis, J., "On the Practical Meaning of Secularism", 73, *Notre Dame Law Review*, 491, 1998.
33. Robbers, G., "Country Report: Federal Republic of Germany on School-Religion Relations", available at http://www.strasbourgconference.org/papers/ On School Religion Relations.pdf, p. 2.

from discriminating between religious communities on grounds of theological or ideological criteria, there is no such prohibition as to treat or support them differently according to their secular performance."[34] According to the German Constitutional Court, state neutrality is compatible with the acknowledgement of Christianity as a formative historical and cultural experience, which may therefore underlie curricula in public education (Decision GER-1975-R-002 a) Germany / b) Federal Constitutional Court / c) First Panel / d) 17-12-1975 / e) 1 BvR 428/69 / f) / g) *Entscheidungen des Bundesverfassungsgerichts* (Official Digest), 41, 65/h)). As the Constitutional Court explained:

> no state, even one that universally guarantees freedom of religion and is committed to religious and ideological neutrality, is in a position completely to divest itself of the cultural and historical values on which social cohesion and the attainment of public goals depend. The Christian religion and the Christian churches have always exerted a tremendous influence in our society, regardless of how this influence is evaluated today. The intellectual traditions rooted in their heritage, the meaning of life and the patterns of behaviour transmitted by them cannot simply be dismissed by the state as irrelevant.[35]

Indeed, when analysing constitutional provisions and jurisprudence on religious freedom, one has to keep in mind that freedom of religion came late to many European democracies, and national constitutions often admittedly record historic compromises. Regard for history and tradition also requires observers to be mindful of the role of religion in the formation of national identities in European polities. As much as the conception of *laïcité* is impossible to fully grasp without being mindful of its role in shaping French republicanism, the state's role in conflicts between new religious movements and traditionally dominant religions cannot be properly

---

34. Heckel, M., "The Impact of Religious Rules on Public Life in Germany", pp. 191-204, in van der Vyver, J. and Witte, J., Jr., eds, *Religious Human Rights in Global Perspective: Legal Perspectives*, Martinus Nijhoff, 1996, pp. 193-197.
35. *Classroom Crucifix II* case, BVerfGE 93, 1. Available in English in Kommers, p. 476. The case is discussed at length in Chapter 3.

understood without reference to the contributions of the dominant faith in shaping the nation and the polity.[36]

The conceptions of *laïcité*, secularity or state neutrality are understood to safeguard and promote tolerance and pluralism in modern European democracies. Proclaiming that tolerance is "the sound foundation of any civil society and of peace," UN GA Resolution 48/126 defines tolerance as "the recognition and appreciation of others, the ability to live together with and to listen to others."[37] While discrimination and intolerance are sometimes used interchangeably, Natan Lerner warns that it is a mistake to treat these terms as synonymous because discrimination in a legal sense does not embrace the entire scope of what is meant by intolerance.[38] In Conor Gearty's words, the "essence of intolerance lies more in the unendureability of an opinion to the listener and in the active hostility that the unacceptability of those opinions then excites. This notion of intolerance is inevitably bound up with the exercise of power by a dominant force."[39]

As the UNESCO Declaration on the Principles of Tolerance (Article 1.1) of 16 November 1995 added, "It is not only a moral duty, it is also a political and legal requirement." Consider the words of Justice Kennedy writing for a majority of the US Supreme Court in *Church of Lukumi Babalu Aye, Inc. v. City of Hialeah*:[40]

> The Free Exercise Clause commits government itself to religious tolerance, and upon even slight suspicion that proposals for state intervention stem from animosity to religion or distrust of its practices, all officials must pause to remember their own high duty to the Constitution and to the rights it

---

36. See, for example, Mojzes, P., "Religious Human Rights in Post-Communist Balkan Countries", pp. 263-284, in van der Vyver, J. and Witte, J., Jr., eds, *Religious Human Rights in Global Perspective, Legal Perspectives*, Martinus Nijhoff, 1996, pp. 270-271.
37. A/RES/48/126, 14 February 1994.
38. Lerner, N., "Religious Human Rights under the United Nations", pp. 79-134, in van der Vyver, J. and Witte, J., Jr., eds, *Religious Human Rights in Global Perspective: Legal Perspectives* (Martinus Nijhoff, 1996), pp. 116-117.
39. Gearty, C. A., "The Internal and External 'Other' in the Union Legal Order, Racism, Religious Intolerance and Xenophobia in Europe", pp. 325-358, in Alston, P., ed., *The EU and Human Rights* (Oxford, 1999), p. 337.
40. *Church of Lukumi Babalu Aye, Inc. v. City of Hialeah*, 508 US 520 (1993), 547.

secures. Those in office must be resolute in resisting importunate demands and must ensure that the sole reasons for imposing the burdens of law and regulation are secular. Legislators may not devise mechanisms, overt or disguised, designed to persecute or oppress a religion or its practices.

Independent of whether or not they retain an official religion or church, European democracies host pluralistic, multi-religious polities. Tensions and conflicts within such polities are unavoidable. In the words of William Galston:

> [p]luralist politics is a politics of recognition rather than that of construction. It respects the diverse sphere of human activity, it does not understand itself as creating or constituting those activities. ... A pluralist politics (is) responsible for co-ordinating other spheres of activity, and especially for adjudicating the inevitable overlaps and disputes among them. This form of politics evidently requires the mutual limitation of some freedoms, individual and associational.[41]

A premise understanding was endorsed by the ECtHR and stated in the *Serif v. Greece* case about the role of the government not being to eliminate pluralism, but "to ensure that the competing groups tolerate each other."[42] The following chapters will explore how far European democracies have advanced on this road.

---

41. Galston, W., "Religion and the Limits of Liberal Democracy", pp. 41-50, in Farrow, D., ed., *Recognizing Religion in a Secular Society, Essays in Pluralism, Religion, and Public Policy*, McGill-Queens, 2004, p. 47.
42. *Serif v. Greece*, Application No. 38178/97, judgment of 14 December 1999, paragraph 53.

Chapter 2
Freedom of religion as an individual right

Although an impressive cohort of international instruments protect freedom of religion, conscience and belief[43] and this freedom appears in the constitutions of virtually all modern democracies, concepts such as religion, conscience or belief tend to withstand lawyerly efforts at establishing a definition.[44] While in cases involving claims based upon free exercise of religious freedom, courts are reluctant to define what amounts to a religion, judicial willingness to provide protection to sincerely held beliefs (whether religious or secular) may result in generous protection to freedom of conscience and religion. In the footsteps of European courts exercising constitutional review, the first part of the chapter provides a general overview on the range of manifestations of religious freedom which is worthy of constitutional protection. Thereafter, the chapter affords a more detailed treatment to two aspects of religious exercise which pose problems that are particularly challenging for constitutionalists: proselytism and conscientious objection to military service. In its account of these issues, the chapter enters into a

---

43. For exceptions, see the constitutions of Belarus (Article 31), Italy (Article 19) and the Netherlands (Article 6(1)).
44. See, for example, Adhar, R. and Leigh, I., *Religious Freedom in the Liberal State*, Oxford, 2005, pp. 110-125, also Gunn, T. J., "The Complexity of Religion and the Definition of 'Religion' in International Law", 16, *Harvard Human Rights Journal*, 189, 2003, and Garay, A., et al., "The Permissible Scope of Legal Limitations on the Freedom of Religion or Belief in France", 19, *Emory International Law Review*, 785, 2005, p. 801.

more detailed, comparative analysis of fundamental constitutional questions concerning religious freedom.

2.1. What amounts to religion or protected belief?

Religious freedom is safeguarded in a number of prominent international human rights instruments and in all European constitutions. Still, in cases involving religious freedoms, courts are rather reluctant to declare whether a particular set or system of ideas, beliefs, teachings or practices constitutes a religion or a creed. Indeed, in a modern secular democracy, passing judgment in matters of faith is not appropriate for governmental bodies, including courts of law. Despite perils surrounding any judicial exercise in defining religion or conscience as such, there are several instances where courts cannot afford to be completely silent about what amounts to religion or secular belief. In cases on free exercise, an important preliminary question for courts to decide is whether the appellant's beliefs are such which merit constitutional protection in the domain of religious freedom.[45] Similar questions arise when courts review governmental decisions on the recognition or registration of religious communities as churches or religious associations, or their eligibility for legal benefits.[46]

In such cases the focus of judicial attention is not on whether the petitioner's convictions amount to "religion" along certain neutral or objective criteria. After all, as Chief Justice Latham of the High Court of Australia observed in his famous decision in *Adelaide Company of Jehovah's Witnesses, Inc. v. The Commonwealth*, "it is not an exaggeration to say that each person chooses the content of his own religion. It is not for a court, upon some a priori basis, to disqualify certain beliefs as incapable of being religious in character."[47] In cases involving religious freedoms, domestic courts tend to focus not, or not solely, on the contents of allegedly religious teachings but on the role those ideas play in an individual's self-

---

45. See, for example, Taylor, P. M., *Freedom of Religion, UN and European Human Rights Law and Practice* (Cambridge, 2005) at 128 et seq. Also Robbers, G., "Religious Freedom in Germany", 2001 *Brigham Young University Law Review*, 643, 2001, p. 663.
46. For more details see Section 3.1.
47. *Adelaide Company of Jehovah's Witnesses, Inc. v. The Commonwealth* (1943) 67 CLR 116, 123-125.

perception.[48] As Justice Iacobucci explained in his judgment for the majority of the Canadian Supreme Court in *Syndicat Northcrest v. Amselem*:

> freedom of religion consists of the freedom to undertake practices and harbour beliefs, having a nexus with religion, in which an individual demonstrates he or she sincerely believes or is sincerely undertaking in order to connect with the divine or as a function of his or her spiritual faith, irrespective of whether a particular practice or belief is required by official religious dogma or is in conformity with the position of religious officials.[49]

In cases involving claims based on religious freedoms, national courts concentrate not on the nature of the beliefs, but on the sincerity of beliefs held by the rights' claimant. Following this route, the US Supreme Court in *U.S. v. Seeger* identified a conviction (religious or not) worthy of constitutional protection under the First Amendment of the US Constitution as a "sincere and meaningful belief which occupies in the life of its possessor a place parallel to that filled by the God of those admittedly qualifying for the exemption comes within the statutory definition."[50] Subsequently, in *Welsh v. U.S.* the US Supreme Court said that the "central consideration in determining whether the registrant's beliefs are religious is whether these beliefs play the role of a religion and function as a religion in the registrant's life."[51] As Gerhard Robbers explains, the German Constitutional Court follows a similar route: "in order to define what a religion is, the self-perception of the relevant believer is of major importance for the Court's decision."[52]

This judicial stance is capable of affording constitutional protection not only to religious beliefs which comply with religious doctrine, but to a much broader set of personal convictions and ideas

---

48. On a typology of judicial techniques used to identify a religious belief's worth of constitutional protection, see Adhar and Leigh, *Religious Freedom in the Liberal State*, pp. 115-125.
49. *Syndicat Northcrest v. Amselem* [2004] 2 S.C.R. 551, 2004 SCC 47, paragraph 46.
50. *U.S. v. Seeger*, 380 U.S. 163 (1965) 176.
51. *Welsh v. U.S*, 398 U.S. 333 (1970), 339.
52. Robbers, *Religious Freedom in Germany*, 2001, p. 663.

– significantly broadening the scope of constitutional protection afforded to religious freedom. As the Austrian Constitutional Court noted, the "identification of behaviour as a religious practice does not depend on whether it complies with binding religious rules, especially since this issue is often subject to debate." (Decision AUT-1950-R-001 a) Austria / b) Constitutional Court / c) / d) 27-09-1950 / e B 72/50; B 92/53; G 9,17/55; B 185,186/58; B 112/59; B 39/70 / f) Freedom of religious worship (freedom to manifest one's beliefs and freedom from external constraints) / g) *Erkenntnisse und Beschlüsse des Verfassungsgerichtshofes* (Official Digest), 2002/1950 of 27.09.1950, 2610/1953 of 14.12.1953, 2944/1955 of 19.12.1955, 3505/1959 of 11.03.1959, 3711/1960 of 25.03.1960, 6919/1972 of 08.12.1972 / h)).

A similar logic permitted the German Constitutional Court to consistently protect such personal convictions of religious believers which were not in line with the teachings of their creed. German constitutional justice accepted a religious applicant's claim to refuse a blood transfusion in a case where the refusal of medical treatment was not commanded by the teachings of the religious community, but was based on the applicant's personal conviction[53] (Decision GER-1971-R-002 a) Germany / b) Federal Constitutional Court / c) First Panel / d) 19-10-1971 / e) 1 BvR 387/65 / f) / g) *Entscheidungen des Bundesverfassungsgerichts* (Official Digest), 32, 98, 266 / h)). More recently, the German Constitutional Court protected the rights of a Turkish Sunni Muslim butcher who – due to competing interpretations concerning slaughtering rituals within the Muslim community[54] – performed halal slaughter without a permit from religious

---

53. The applicant referred to the common prayer for the sick person.
54. The Muslim Council in Germany regarded the rites performed by the Turkish butcher necessary, although according to a Sunni Muslim expert in Cairo (consulted by the lower administrative court), the rites were not required by religion.
    A similar problem about ritual slaughter also arose in France within the Jewish community where only those Jewish associations may receive a permit to conduct ritual slaughter which are approved by the Israelite Consistory of France. Described in Garay, A. et al., "The Permissible Scope of Legal Limitations on the Freedom of Religion or Belief in France", 19, *Emory International Law Review*, 785, 2005, note 69 on p. 798. The claim of the organisation which did not receive a permit reached the ECtHR in *Cha'are Shalom Ve Tsedek v. France*, Application No. 27417/95, Judgment of 27 June 2000, discussed in detail below.

authorities.[55] When finding that under the Basic Law the applicant butcher had a right to exercise his vocation in a particular manner, it was instrumental for German constitutional justices that the Muslim community affected in the case sincerely believed in the propriety of ritual slaughter in the manner as it was performed by the applicant. Thus, while protecting unique personal convictions in these cases, the German Constitutional Court provided an example for the protection of freedom of conscience independent of the teachings or doctrines of a particular religion. In addition, as Edward Eberle notes, the decision of the German Constitutional Court in the ritual slaughter case "recognised a diversity of belief within the Islamic community."[56]

In addition to protecting religious beliefs, international instruments and constitutions also provide protection to secular convictions. Throughout Europe, among non-religious convictions seeking constitutional protection one may often find claims by atheists, humanists and pacifists. The German Constitutional Court explained the relationship of protecting personal convictions and religious beliefs in one of its early decisions in the following words:

> The fundamental right to the free exercise of religion is included within the concept of freedom of belief. ... At least since the Weimar Constitution the right to free exercise of religion has been merged with the freedom of belief. ... The right to free exercise extends not only to Christian churches but also to other religious creeds and ideological associations ... Thus there is no justification for interpreting the freedom to perform the rituals associated with religious belief more narrowly than freedom of belief or creed.[57]

Some might find it disappointing that the jurisprudence of Strasbourg rights protection fora offers much less guidance on what amounts to religion or belief for the purposes of the application

---

55. BVerfGE 104, 337. The full text of the decision is available as an English translation at http://www.bundesverfassungsgericht.de/entscheidungen/rs20020115_1bvr178399en.html
56. Eberle, E., "Free Exercise of Religion in Germany and the United States", 78, *Tulane Law Review* 1023, 2004, p. 1058.
57. *Rumpelkammer case*, BVerfGE 24, 236, 1968). Available in English in Kommers, D. P., *The Constitutional Jurisprudence of the Federal Republic of Germany*, Duke, 1997, second edition, p. 444.

of Article 9. In an early case where the European Commission of Human Rights first had to decide whether the applicant's rights were protected under Article 9 of the Convention, the Commission said that while the applicant's desired action has "a strong personal motivation", nonetheless, it does not amount to a "manifestation of any belief in the sense that some coherent view on fundamental problems can be seen as being expressed thereby."[58] The European Court of Human Rights (ECtHR) is similarly reluctant to establish a test for deciding whether a set of beliefs amounts to religion for the purposes of rights protection. Instead, the ECtHR is satisfied with accepting a belief if it attains a "certain level of cogency, seriousness, cohesion and importance."[59] Permissive as it may appear, in practice this standard is not trivial to meet. In *Pretty v. the United Kingdom*, the ECtHR said, for instance, that although it does not question "the firmness of the applicant's views concerning assisted suicide (these views) do not involve a form of manifestation of a religion or belief, through worship, teaching, practice or observance as described [in the Convention]. To the extent that the applicant's views reflect her commitment to the principle of personal autonomy, her claim is a restatement of the complaint raised under Article 8 of the Convention."[60]

As a consequence, petitioners who claim protection for secular or individualised convictions or beliefs easily run into difficulties before Strasbourg institutions under Article 9 of the ECHR. The problems are well illustrated by a decision in *Arrowsmith v. the United Kingdom*, where the majority of the European Commission found that while pacifism was a "belief based on thought and conscience" worthy of protection under Article 9.1, the contents

---

58. *X. v. Germany*, Application No. 8741/1979, 24 DR 137, p. 138.
59. As in *Campbell and Cosans v. United Kingdom*, Application No. 7511/76 and No. 7743/76 [1982], judgment of 25 February 1982 (definition of belief under Article 2 of Protocol No. 1). See, also, Evans, C., "Religious Freedom in European Human Rights Law: The Search for a Guiding Conception", pp. 385-400, in Janis, M. W. and Evans, C., eds, *Religion and International Law*, Martinus Nijhoff, 2004, p. 390.
60. *Pretty v. the United Kingdom*, Application No. 2346/02, Judgment of 29 April 2002, paragraph 82. For a similar conclusion see *Johnston v. Ireland*, Application No. 9697/82, Judgment of 18 December 1986, rejecting a contention that Ireland's prohibition of belief violates applicant freedom of belief, while warning that Article 9 cannot be used to create a right to divorce.

of the leaflets distributed by the pacifist applicant giving rise to the case did not constitute practice of a belief under Article 9.1.[61] Under criteria applied in *Arrowsmith*, petitioners were required to show before both the Commission and the ECtHR that their conduct (or a restricted action) was required by their religion or belief. This "necessity" test turned out fairly unpredictable and difficult for applicants to surpass.[62] To the extent beholders of lesser known faiths and secular convictions might exercise their freedoms, they might still find it challenging to find protection for their conduct recognised as a practice worthy of protection under Article 9. As a major reason why the ECtHR is being cautious about protecting personal convictions, Carolyn Evans cites the potential for abuse in receiving privileges to which the application would otherwise not be entitled (e.g. in the context of prisons).[63]

2.2. The scope of *forum internum* and protected manifestations of freedom of religion

The protection of the inner core of conscience (*forum internum*) from any governmental interference in absolute terms was explained in the Krishnaswami study in the following terms: "Freedom to maintain or to change religion or belief falls primarily within the domain of the inner faith and conscience of an individual. Viewed from this angle, one would assume that any intervention from outside is not only illegitimate but impossible."[64] Aspects of religious freedom which fall within the *forum internum* therefore may not be subject to limitation or restriction. Although there is no agreement between commentators as to how far the *forum internum* extends and what exactly falls within its boundaries past the freedom to choose, maintain and change one's religion, there is a

---

61. *Arrowsmith v. United Kingdom*, Application No. 7050/75, Comm. Rep 1978, 19 DR 5.
62. For a detailed, critical analysis of the Arrowsmith "necessity" test see Evans, C., *Freedom of Religion under the European Convention on Human Rights*, Oxford, 2001, pp. 115 et seq.
63. Evans, C., *Religious Freedom in European Human Rights Law*, p. 391.
64. Krishnaswami, A., *Study of Discrimination in the Matter of Religious Rights and Practices*, UN Doc. E/CN.4/Sub.2/200/Rev.1, UN Sales No. 60. XIV.2, available at: http://www.religlaw.org/interdocs/docs/akstudy1960.htm.

clear agreement that the decisions comprising the *forum internum* should be free from coercion.[65]

Activities which fall outside this *forum internum*, understood as external "manifestations" of religious freedom in the human rights parlance, are, however, subject to limitations within constitutional boundaries. The exercise of religious freedom takes place in a wide variety of forms. As much as the proper scope of the *forum internum* is difficult to delineate, protected manifestations of freedom of religion are also impossible to list with precision. National constitutions differ in how detailed a catalogue they offer. A useful, albeit not definitive,[66] account on the most prominent manifestations of religious freedom is contained in Article 6 of the 1981 Declaration on the Elimination of All Forms of Intolerance and of Discrimination Based on Religion or Belief[67] offering the following list of freedoms comprising free religious exercise:

> a. To worship or assemble in connection with a religion or belief, and to establish and maintain places for these purposes;
>
> b. To establish and maintain appropriate charitable or humanitarian institutions;
>
> c. To make, acquire and use to an adequate extent the necessary articles and materials related to the rites or customs of a religion or belief;
>
> d. To write, issue and disseminate relevant publications in these areas;
>
> e. To teach a religion or belief in places suitable for these purposes;

---

65. For a review of views, see Taylor, *Freedom of Religion*, pp. 116 et seq.
66. Lerner, N., "Religious Human Rights under the United Nations", pp. 79-134, in van der Vyver, J. and Witte, J., Jr., eds., *Religious Human Rights in Global Perspective: Legal Perspectives*, Martinus Nijhoff, 1996, pp. 118-119 reminds us that although this list is strongly influenced by the findings of the Krishnaswami study, it should be taken as a minimum standard, as it does not include many rights, some of which were excluded already in the drafting process.
67. Proclaimed by General Assembly Resolution 36/55 of 25 November 1981.

f. To solicit and receive voluntary financial and other contributions from individuals and institutions;

g. To train, appoint, elect or designate by succession appropriate leaders called for by the requirements and standards of any religion or belief;

h. To observe days of rest and to celebrate holidays and ceremonies in accordance with the precepts of one's religion or belief;

i. To establish and maintain communications with individuals and communities in matters of religion and belief at the national and international levels.

Unlike the *forum internum*, external manifestations of religious freedom may be subject to limitations. Certainly, national constitutions may prescribe the range of permissible limitations of religious freedom more narrowly than is defined in Article 9.2 of the ECHR.

A note on terminology and the helpfulness of abstract delineations is in place here. On its face, a distinction reminiscent of the one between *forum internum* and manifestations of religion has been drawn in US constitutional jurisprudence in *Reynolds v. U.S.*,[68] when Chief Justice Waite assured that "laws are made for the government of actions and while they cannot interfere with belief and opinions, they may with practices." Note however, that this approach leaves very little protection for the external manifestations of religious freedom (i.e. action) against governmental interference. Although the US Supreme Court appeared to be abandoning this approach, the court was seen to return to it more recently. In *Employment Division v. Smith*, the Supreme Court also affirmed that the threshold of justification for governmental action restricting behaviour motivated by religious belief is below the strict scrutiny test used in constitutional cases involving limitations on fundamental rights.[69] Note also that, a different approach on freedom of religion familiar in French constitutional scholarship associates religious freedom with the internal aspects of religion. In this reading external manifestations of religious freedom are understood to

---

68. *Reynolds v. U.S.*, 98 US 145 (1878), paragraph 166.
69. *Employment Division, Department of Human Resources of the State of Oregon, et al. v. Smith*, 494 US 872 (1990).

belong in the terrain of the liberties of religious associations ("*la liberté des cultes*") where religious liberty is exercised in a community with others.[70]

The following commentary cannot concentrate on all aspects of religious freedom worthy of constitutional protection. Therefore, the discussion will focus on a few select points which are illustrative of basic constitutional dilemmas regarding the *forum internum* and manifestations of religious freedom. The problems selected intend to provide an overview on courts' efforts to define the scope of the *forum internum* and permissible limitations imposed on manifestations of religious freedom as an individual right.

> ### Case law
>
> - AUT-1950-R-001 a) Austria / b) Constitutional Court / c) / d) 27-09-1950 / e) B 72/50; B 92/53; G 9,17/55; B 185,186/58; B 112/59; B 39/70 / f) Freedom of religious worship (freedom to manifest one's beliefs and freedom from external constraints) / g) *Erkenntnisse und Beschlüsse des Verfassungsgerichtshofes* (Official Digest), 2002/1950 of 27.09.1950, 2610/1953 of 14.12.1953, 2944/1955 of 19.12.1955, 3505/1959 of 11.03.1959, 3711/1960 of 25.03.1960, 6919/1972 of 08.12.1972 / h)
>
> As well as providing for freedom of religion, conscience and personal belief, the Austrian Constitution – which applies a liberal definition of fundamental rights – protects the right to practise a religion and to manifest one's personal beliefs. This is known as "*Weltanschauungspflege*" (exercise of personal beliefs) or "freedom of worship" in the broad sense. It encompasses "freedom of worship" in the narrow sense as well as "freedom of religion". Whereas the former refers to belief-oriented activities bearing some relation to an event such as a religious ritual and implying the establishment of at least a

---

70. See, for example, Claude-Albert Colliard and Rosaline Letteron, *Libertés publiques*, Dalloz, 2005, eighth edition, p. 427.
In English, Robert, J., "Religious Liberty and French Secularism", 2003, *Brigham Young University Law Review*, 637, 2003, pp. 649-650 and Garay, A., et al., "The Permissible Scope of Legal Limitations on the Freedom of Religion or Belief in France", 19, *Emory International Law Review*, 785, 2005, pp. 801-802.

primitive form of religion (VfSlg. 2002/1950, 2610/1953), the latter includes all other manifestations of belief, regardless of whether they concern private or public behaviour. Every inhabitant of Austria has the right, in public or in private and alone or in community with others, to manifest or practise freely any kind of belief, religion or denomination (Article 63.2 of the State Treaty of St Germain, StGBl 1920/303, Article 9, ECHR). The right to practise a religion both in private and in public is not confined to followers of recognised religions or members of recognised religious communities (VfSlg. 6919/1972).

Religious practice takes a number of forms (conducting and participating in worship, conducting services, administering and receiving sacraments at religious ceremonies to mark specific occasions such as weddings and funerals, meditation, processions, verbal expressions of religious belief, distribution of tracts or presentation of works of religious art, speeches on religious themes, education and upbringing) ... Religious practices include religious customs such as the ringing of bells during a service, the wearing of religious clothing and animal sacrifices as part of the observance of certain religions ... The right to manifest one's religious beliefs also includes the freedom not to do so and the freedom to manifest non-religious personal beliefs such as pacifist convictions.

The Constitution therefore does not guarantee unrestricted freedom of worship. The manifestation of various personal beliefs must be consistent with public order and morals (Article 63 of the State Treaty of St Germain). In particular, freedom of worship is subject to the statutory restrictions provided for in Article 9.2, ECHR; such restrictions are allowed on grounds of public safety, public order, health, morals and protection of the rights and freedoms of others ...

- SVK-1995-2-005 a) Slovakia / b) Constitutional Court / c) Plenary / d) 24-05-1995 / e) PL. US 18/95 / f) Case of unconstitutional restriction of religious faith in relationship to the military service / g) *Zbierka nálezov a uznesení Ústavného súdu Slovenskej republiky* (Official Digest), 1995, 171-189 / h) Codices (Slovak)

> The right to change one's mind over one's religion or faith which is implied in freedom of thought, etc. is a component of *forum internum* and for this reason it is absolute and unrestrictable. No one may be forced to change his/her religion and faith, or to adopt a confession ...
>
> However, the real value of these absolute as well as unrestrictable freedoms can, in some cases only, be offered to the entitled persons if they manifest their right publicly. The right to express thought, religion and faith is guaranteed by the last sentence of Article 24.1 of the Constitution. The word "opinion" used in this sentence must be interpreted in the context of Article 24.1 of the Constitution as any public expression by a human being, of their thoughts, conscience, religion or faith. It is only natural that the spectrum of those external expressions is very broad and heterogeneous, and precise legal effects are attached to some of them e.g. the church marriage.
>
> Public expressions in which the freedoms guaranteed under Article 24.1 of the Constitution are exercised may be restricted by Acts of Parliament, if the terms of Article 24.4 of the Constitution are met. All kinds of expressions protected through Article 24.1 of the Constitution may be restricted equally. That means there is no constitutional difference between thoughts, conscience, religion and faith. This is so as the Constitution provides no exception for probable restrictions imposed on thoughts, conscience, religion and faith.

Commentary

Interference with the *forum internum?*
Revealing convictions: registration of religious affiliation

In modern governments heavy with bureaucratic procedures, registration of religious affiliation might appear as a seemingly minor and harmless interference with freedom of conscience. Just taking the narrow perspective of religious freedom on governmental operations, consider that without some record it is difficult to imagine an efficient distribution of government funding for religious activities or the operation of a system of religious education. The German Constitutional Court, for instance, finds the registration of one's religious identity with the tax authorities acceptable for the purposes of the collection and distribution of church taxes, as registration ensures the "orderly collection of church taxes by the state ... on behalf of religious communities." (Decision GER-1978-R-001 a) Germany / b) Federal Constitutional Court / c) First Panel / d) 23-10-1978 / e) 1 BvR 439/75 / f) / g) *Entscheidungen des Bundesverfassungsgerichts* (Official Digest), 49, 375 / h)).[71]

Making such a record, however, is based on revealing or determining one's (actual or assumed) creed. Admitting to holding (or not holding) a faith or belief is a gesture that exposes an individual's most private affairs. Harris, O'Boyle and Warbrick go as far as saying that "there is no good reason why the state needs the information (though there are bad ones)."[72] Several European constitutions[73] and data protection laws[74] contain express prohibitions on requiring or compelling someone to reveal their faith (religion). Such constitutional and legal provisions are in line with General Comment No. 22 submitting that "no one can be compelled to

---

71. See also GER-1977-R-001. (a) Germany; (b) Federal Constitutional Court; (c) First Panel; (d) 25-10-1977; (e) 1 BvR 323/75; (f); (g) *Entscheidungen des Bundesverfassungsgerichts* (Official Digest), 46, 266; (h) where the German Constitutional Court held that it was appropriate to request patients to reveal their faiths, as long as they are informed that it is not mandatory to answer this question.
72. Harris, D. J., O'Boyle, M. and Warbrick, C., *Law of the European Convention on Human Rights*, Butterworths, 1995, second edition, p. 361.
73. See, for example, Polish Constitution (53.7), Russian Constitution (Article 29(3)), Slovene Constitution (Article 41.2), Spanish Constitution (Article 16.2), Swedish Constitution (Article 2), Turkish Constitution (Article 15.2). The Portuguese Constitution provides that information on religious affiliation may only be gathered as statistical information (Article 41.3) and expressly prohibits storing data on religious affiliation in a computerised form (Article 35.3).
74. Collection, processing and storage of data on religious affiliation may also be proscribed in data protection laws. For example, Hungarian Act No. 63 of 1992 on the Protection of Personal Data and Public Access to Data of Public Interest, Articles 2.2 and 30.b. For an English translation see: http://abiweb.obh.hu/dpc/legislation/1992_LXIIIa.htm. See also the Spanish prohibition on the collection of census data on religious affiliation. Article 7, Organic Law 15/1999 of 13 December on the Protection of Personal Data. An unofficial English translation of the act is available at http://ec.europa.eu/justice_home/fsj/privacy/docs/organic-law-99.pdf.

reveal his thoughts or adherence to a religion or belief."[75] Note, however, that restrictions on the collection and processing of data concerning religious affiliations are not at all universal and constitutional review fora are also not in agreement about the nature and intensity of such governmental action. Differences between national constitutions and disagreement between courts highlight important nuances not only about conceptions on the *forum internum* but also about courts' perceptions of governmental interference with individual autonomy.

According to the Greek Council of State "no one may be obliged by any means to reveal, directly or indirectly, their religion or religious convictions; consequently, no one may be obliged to act or refrain from acting in ways that could serve as a basis for presumptions regarding the existence or otherwise of these convictions." Therefore, it found the inclusion of religious affiliation on identity cards, on a mandatory basis, to be unconstitutional, while acknowledging that individuals might have to reveal their religious affiliation in order to exercise their religious freedom (e.g. in order to file for conscientious objector status). The Council of State reasoned that the voluntary inclusion of religious affiliation on governmental documents is also unacceptable. According to the Greek Council of State:

> the opposite interpretation would lead to infringement of the negative form of religious freedom for those Greek citizens who do not wish to express their religious convictions in this way, and remove the state's religious neutrality as regards the exercise of this freedom. ... In practice, Greek citizens who are opposed to a reference to their religion or religious convictions on their identity card would be obliged, indirectly and to all intents and purposes publicly, to reveal an aspect of their personal religious convictions, especially since refusal to have this reference included would be recorded by the public bodies on a state document that is submitted as a means of identification to any authority or department, or to any individual. ... the mention of religion on identity cards provides grounds for possible discrimination, favourable or unfavourable, and thus carries the risk that it may infringe

---

75. General Comment No. 22: *The right to freedom of thought, conscience and religion*, Article 18, 30/07/93. CCPR/C/21/Rev.1/Add. (1993), paragraph 3.

the religious equality (Decision GRE-2001-2-001 a) Greece / b) Council of State / c) Assembly / d) 27-06-2001 / e) 2283/2001 / f) / g) / h)).

The decision of the Greek Council of State on the optional inclusion of religious affiliation on identity cards came after, in 2000, the Greek government was pressured to remove reference to one's religious beliefs from the cards altogether. The Orthodox Church opposed the government's decision and engaged in a mass mobilisation campaign, enjoying the support of the majority of the population according to public opinion polls. An interesting factor underlying the entire debate is that in Greek "the same word (*tavtotita*) means both 'identity' and 'identity card'. Hence, the proposal to eliminate religion from the identity card registers with listeners as meaning the elimination of religion from their identity."[76]

Moving in the opposite direction, the Turkish Constitutional Court found the inclusion of religious identity on identity cards to be compatible with the requirements of secularism and the separation of church and state.[77] This finding is at least surprising in the light of the fact that Article 15.2 of the Turkish Constitution provides that "no one may be compelled to reveal his religion, conscience, thought or opinion, nor be accused on account of them," a prohibition which applies also at the time of war and emergency. The inclusion of religious affiliation on identity cards is of special concern in Turkey for the Ba'hai who are unable to state their religion as it is not included among the options. Under the new Personal Status Law enacted in 2006, citizens may request the removal of their religion from their official records (Article 35.2), the law at

---

76. Verney, S., "Challenges to Greek Identity", 1.2, *European Political Science*, pp. 12-16, 2002, also at http://www.essex.ac.uk/ecpr/publications/eps/onlineissues/spring2002/features/verney.htm. For a discussion of politics behind the Greek identity card conundrum see George T. Mavrogordatos, "Orthodoxy and Nationalism in the Greek Case", pp. 117-136, in Madeley, J. T. S. and Enyedi, Zs., eds., *Church and State in Contemporary Europe, The Chimera of Neutrality*, Frank Cass, 2003, pp. 122-123.
77. Described at Belge, C., "Friends of the Court: The Republican Alliance and Selective Activism of the Constitutional Court of Turkey", 40, *Law and Society Review*, 653, 2006, p. 675.

another place, however, still requires Turkish citizens to provide information on their religious affiliation (Article 7.1.e).[78]

Certainly, it would be a mistake to assume that all legal solutions on registering religious affiliation are based upon compulsion or coercion. Also, while there is a clear difference between registration systems which are mandatory and the ones which are optional, before expressing a clear preference for the latter regime one has to investigate the purpose and consequences of registration within a specific legal system. The element of free choice informing voluntary systems of registration might easily vanish if refusal of registration is most likely to trigger mistreatment or denial of access to otherwise vital services. Thus, when evaluating the constitutionality of a registration scheme – may this exercise take place solely with reference to religious freedom or should it also be sensitive to considerations about discrimination or data protection – courts should be mindful of the fact that formalities of a registration process may hinder individuals from professing a creed of their choice and as such, may interfere with the inviolable core of religious freedom.

Refusing to take an oath: A decision within the *forum internum* or a proper manifestation of religious freedom?

Constitutional court decisions concerning the right to refuse to take an oath on grounds of conscience present excellent illustrations on how difficult it is to draw a line between cases concerning the scope of the *forum internum* and instances where the permissible limitations of the manifestation of religious freedom are at stake. Furthermore, on account of these cases it is easy to demonstrate how judicial assessment of limitations imposed upon religious freedom border on arguments about coercion in matters of faith. The latter aspect of these cases is particularly interesting as it foreshadows difficulties in distinguishing problems in cases about the impermissible imposition of a state's preferences about religion, problems which are discussed in the following section concerning days of rest and religious holidays.

---

78. Oehring, O., "Turkey: Little Progress on Religious Freedom", at: http://www.forum18.org/Archive.php?article_id=817. Oehring adds: "Changing religious affiliation on an individual's personal records was possible before, but required an individual to do this through the courts. Fear of social ostracism or hostility meant that few did this."

Few constitutions contain express provisions on religious oaths.[79] Article 192 of the Belgian Constitution provides that no one may be coerced to take an oath, unless prescribed by law. The first Belgian law entrenching this constitutional provision provided a variety of formulations, all containing the phrase "so help me God." In 1867 the Cour de Cassation was of the view that the reference to God in such an oath is inevitable and therefore the law does not violate religious freedom. This law was amended as late as in 1974. Although the new law no longer refers to God, it still does not provide an opportunity to refuse an oath altogether. When Jehovah's Witnesses refused to take a secular oath and challenged the law in 2000, a lower court judge said that since God is not mentioned in the text of the law, an oath cannot be refused with reference to religious freedom.[80] In a more recent decision, the Court of Arbitration ruled that a public servant cannot refuse to swear allegiance to the King with reference to freedom of opinion (i.e. secular convictions), because "the oath was of as much interest to those who heard it as to those who took it." (Decision BEL-2002-3-009 a) Belgium / b) Court of Arbitration / c) / d) 15-10-2002 / e) 151/2002 / f) / g) *Moniteur belge* (Official Gazette), 10.02.2003 / h) Codices (French, German, Dutch)).

The Greek Constitution also provides that no oath may be taken or imposed against one's religious convictions (Article 13.5). When the Greek Council of State agreed to release a student from taking an oath as a condition of obtaining a master's degree, the Council agreed that:

> [the student] may instead make a solemn promise referring to his or her honour or conscience, even where such an

---

79. The German Basic Law provides in Article 56 that the oath for taking a seat in Parliament may be sworn without the religious affirmation. Compare with the Greek Constitution saying in Article 59.2 that all MPs shall take an oath according to their own religion.

80. Torfs, R., "On the Permissible Scope of Legal Limitations on the Freedom of Religion or Belief in Belgium", 19, *Emory International Law Review*, 637 (2005), at pp. 656-657. Cf. GER-1972-R-001 a) Germany / b) Federal Constitutional Court / c) Second Panel / d) 11-04-1972 / e) 2 BvR 75/71 / f) / g) *Entscheidungen des Bundesverfassungsgerichts* (Official Digest), 33, 23 / h), holding that "Beliefs which lead their holders to refuse, for religious reasons, to swear even an oath which does not invoke God are protected by Article 4.1 of the Basic Law."

affirmation is not provided for by law as a substitute for the religious oath. However, the person concerned must state the religion that he or she professes, the principles of which prohibit him/her from taking an oath, or state that he or she is a non-believer or atheist. This declaration is not contrary to freedom of religion, as it is necessary in order to release the individual from an obligation that would conflict with his or her religious beliefs (Decision GRE-1998-R-002 a) Greece / b) Council of State / c) 6th Section / d) 18-06-1998 / e) 2601/98 / f) / g) / h)).

Note that if taking an oath is characterised not as an aspect of the *forum internum* but as a manifestation of religious freedom one may wonder what may amount to a constitutionally acceptable limitation thereupon. Furthermore, the pre-condition of making a "solemn promise" instead of a religious oath is also problematic, to the extent that it, in effect, compels a student to reveal their faith – an act which seems to run counter to the inviolability of the *forum internum*.

The Italian Constitutional Court was also willing to provide an exemption on religious grounds from taking an oath in criminal and subsequently also in civil cases. Unlike the Greek Council of State, however, the Italian Constitutional Court relied not so much on the applicant's freedom of conscience or religious freedom, but on constitutional requirements controlling the activities of a secular state (Decision ITA-1995-2-008 a) Italy / b) Constitutional Court / c) / d) 04-05-1995 / e) 149/1995 / f) / g) *Gazzetta Ufficiale, Prima Serie Speciale* (Official Gazette), 19, 10.05.1995 / h) Codices (Italian) and ITA-1996-R-001 a) Italy / b) Constitutional Court / c) / d) 30-09-1996 / e) 334/1996 / f) / g) *Gazzetta Ufficiale, Prima Serie Speciale* (Official Gazette), 42, 16.10.1996 / h)). This approach is different from the one in the Greek case, as it removes the problem from the terrain of free exercise jurisprudence, and replaces it with questions about the proper role of the state in matters of faith.

This trail of argument focusing on the position of the state was developed even further in the US Supreme Court's decision in *Torcaso v. Watkins*, a case concerning the constitutionality of an oath requiring a notary public in the state of Maryland to declare his belief in God. Justice Black writing for the court said that:

> neither a State nor the Federal Government can constitutionally force a person "to profess a belief or disbelief in any

religion." Neither can constitutionally pass laws or impose requirements which aid all religions as against non-believers, and neither can aid those religions based on a belief in the existence of God as against those religions founded on different beliefs.[81]

In a similar fashion, the ECtHR found in *Buscarini and others v. San Marino*,[82] that – despite the history and traditions of Christianity in San Marino, and the government's wide margin of appreciation – an oath required of members of the San Marinese parliament, sworn on the "Holy Gospels" violates religious freedom under Article 9. The ECtHR warned that "it would be contradictory to make the exercise of a mandate intended to represent different views of society within Parliament subject to a prior declaration of commitment to a particular set of beliefs."[83]

An interesting aspect of the Italian, US and ECtHR decisions – which puts them in sharp contrast with the Greek case – is the way the courts approached the constitutional problem. While the Greek Council of State understood the oath requirement as a limitation on free exercise, and thus was willing to concede to certain limitations (note the requirement of precisely stating one's beliefs which stop them taking an oath), the other courts understood a religious oath as an instance of governmental imposition (establishment) of religious beliefs. If understood so, individuals' religious freedom to be free from coercion in matters of conscience prevails against religious oath requirements imposed by legislation.[84]

---

81. *Torcaso v. Watkins*, 367 US 488 (1961), 495.
82. *Buscarini and others v. San Marino*, Application No. 24645/94, judgment of 18 February 1999.
83. *Buscarini and others v. San Marino*, paragraph 39. Note that according to Taylor the ECtHR erred when taking the case as one on the manifestation of religion instead of a matter about the *forum internum* (which permits no limitation). See Taylor, *Freedom of Religion*, pp. 129-130.
84. Note, however, that a secular oath is difficult to refuse upon grounds of freedom of conscience. See the Spanish Constitutional Tribunal's decision (RTC 1983/101, 18 Nov. 1983) summarised in English in Dorsen, N. et al., *Comparative Constitutionalism*, West, 2001, p. 945.

Religious holiday, Sunday laws and faith-based days of rest: proper limitations on manifestation of religious freedom, coercion in matter of faith or imposition of a state's religious preferences

Several religions require their followers to celebrate certain days or even longer periods as holidays (feasts) and also to take rest on certain days of the week. In modern states where a secular calendar also prescribes public holidays and regular days of rest, the secular calendar is almost bound to clash with the requirements of at least some religious calendars and regulations. While the state's complete abstention from turning religious holidays into public holidays is most desirable in a neutral and secular state, even the most secular European governments tend to acknowledge at least a few holidays which have religious origins. Providing an opportunity for the observation of all religious holidays in the form of a public holiday presents a special problem in multi-ethnic and multi-religious polities, as granting governmental recognition to all major holidays of all religions present in the country is simply impracticable. Recognition of the majority's holy days is acceptable, as long as the minorities' days are also duly protected.[85] Problems arise when the government appears to prefer certain creeds over others. Furthermore, religions differ not only in singling out particular days of the week as a regular (periodic) day of rest, but also in the intensity of their requirements about the proper observance of that day (with religious requirements ranging from the prohibition of certain activities to requiring the performance of certain duties or ceremonies). Thus, in observance of religious rules believers of certain creeds may wish to refuse to work at times which are otherwise not secular days of rest or holidays.

Cases arising from such conflicts present important opportunities to analyse the willingness of courts to protect believers and non-believers against coercion in matters of faith, and also to foster accommodation of believers' needs. Judicial decisions provide ample opportunity to reflect on the proximity of arguments about free religious exercise and the imposition of a state's preferences in matters of religion (endorsement, or establishment of a religion, to use the US terminology). Such cases are especially interesting as

---

85. Lerner, *Religious Human Rights under the United Nations*, pp. 120-121.

few constitutions contain express provisions on days of rest and religious holidays.[86]

The case in which the potential for an interference with the *forum internum* is probably the most prevalent surfaced both before the Macedonian Constitutional Court and subsequently before the ECtHR. The decision centres on the fate of an employee, who was known to observe Christian holidays, yet did not report for work on two Muslim holidays – claiming that he was a convert to Islam.[87] The Macedonian domestic courts were most concerned about the sincerity of the applicant's beliefs. Due to the petitioner's failure to establish what the Constitutional Court called the "objective facts" underscoring his complaint, the Constitutional Court found that the petitioner's religious freedom was not violated (Decision MKD-2000-2-005 a) "The former Yugoslav Republic of Macedonia" / b) Constitutional Court / c) / d) 12-07-2000 / e) U.br.220/99 / f) / g) *Sluzben vesnik na Republika Makedonija* (Official Gazette), 57/2000 / h) Codices (Macedonian). When the same case reached the ECtHR in *Kosteski v. The former Yugoslav Republic of Macedonia*, the ECtHR said the following in the course of Article 9 analysis:

> In the context of employment, with contracts setting out specific obligations and rights between employer and employee, the Court does not find it unreasonable that an employer may regard absence without permission or apparent justification as a disciplinary matter. Where the employee then seeks to rely on a particular exemption, it is not oppressive or in fundamental conflict with freedom of conscience to require some level of substantiation when that claim concerns a privilege or entitlement not commonly available and, if that substantiation is not forthcoming, to reach a negative conclusion.[88]

---

86. Among these few is the German Basic Law in Article 140 incorporating Article 139 of the Weimar Constitution which provides that Sundays and feast days shall be days of rest. See also the Belgian Constitution which contains a right not to participate in religious ceremonies and – in particular – not to observe days of rest (Article 20).
87. The exemption permitting the observance of Muslim holidays was in a statute.
88. *Kosteski v. the former Yugoslav Republic of Macedonia*, Application No. 55170/00, judgment of 13 April 2006, paragraph 39.

Thus, while the case on its face concerns the right to observe the holidays of one's professed religion (a manifestation of religious freedom), courts of law were halted at the preliminary issue of ascertaining the sincerity of the petitioner's beliefs. It seems to receive little judicial attention, however, that testing the sincerity of one's beliefs is not a simple technicality but might amount to an interference with the *forum internum*. Among many other considerations (e.g. lack of objective conditions and sound evidence) it is for this latter reason that developing a test is particularly challenging. In the case of such difficulties, and acknowledging that evidence on insincerity would differ from case to case, Carolyn Evans suggests that in cases where a fraud is suspected, the "burden of proof should be on the state to show some reason to think that the person is using religious or other belief fraudulently in order to obtain an advantage to which he or she would not be otherwise entitled."[89]

Legislation and subsequent court decisions on public holidays coinciding with major religious holidays are often seen as being indicators of political and judicial willingness to endorse certain (preferred or prevailing) religions over others. Acknowledging that the governmental recognition of religious holidays amounts to improper endorsement, the Supreme Court of Mozambique declared a calendar of public holidays which consists solely of Islamic religious holidays violates religious freedom and equality before the law. In this case, the Supreme Court emphasised that "to decree a religious holiday as a public holiday is more than accommodating the activities of that religion; it is placing a value on the religion and granting it a special status that other religions do not have. ... [It] does not contribute to the promotion of a climate of understanding and social tolerance ... It might even cause a focus of social discord and lead to religious intolerance ..." (Decision MOZ-1996-D-001 a) Mozambique / b) Supreme Court / c) / d) 27-12-1996 / e) / f) Preventive analysis of the constitutionality of the law proclaiming Islamic religious holidays as public holidays (Ide-Ul-Fitre and Ide-Ul-Adha) / g) *Boletim da República*, III Série, N.º 49, de 04 de Dezembro de 2002 / h) Codices (Portuguese)).

---

89. Evans, C., *Freedom of Religion*, p. 59.

The Hungarian Constitutional Court was not sensitive to symbolic significance the roster of public holidays might have in the eyes of many who consider official holidays a mirror on the history, traditions and identity of a polity. When leaders of the Jewish religious community approached the Hungarian Constitutional Court, complaining that the most important Jewish holidays were not Hungarian public (official) holidays, constitutional justice found that the "most important holidays of the Christian religions nowadays have a secularised and general social character. They are special days not because of their religious content but because of economic considerations and because they comply with the expectations of society" (Decision HUN-1993-1-004 a) Hungary / b) Constitutional Court / c) / d) 27-02-1993 / e) 10/1993 / f) Saturday Work Case / g) *Magyar Közlöny* (Official Gazette), 22/1993 / h) Codices (Hungarian). To the extent the reasoning of the Hungarian Constitutional Court emphasises the lack of impact Jewish holidays made on Hungarian public life and culture, the Hungarian decision can be seen as excluding certain religious communities from the definition of the polity for the purposes of constitutional analysis. Such a stance is hardly compatible with the requirements of state neutrality in a constitutional democracy.[90]

The argument on the secularisation of certain, formerly religious days of rest is very familiar from judicial decisions on Sunday laws. In its judgment in *McGowan v. Maryland*[91] the US Supreme Court famously upheld a Sunday closing law against a challenge under the Establishment Clause of the First Amendment, finding that the purpose of the Sunday closing rule was secular, as it aimed to establish a uniform day of rest. In a similar logic, when a Seventh Day Adventist was refused an early shift by his employer which would have made it possible for him to observe Sabbath, the European Commission was satisfied with finding that all religious communities

---

90. Beyond their symbolic significance legal rules adjusting a public calendar to religious holidays may also interfere with the exercise of other constitutional rights. For example, in TUR-1993-1-001 a) Turkey / b) Constitutional Court / c) / d) 20-01-1993 / e) E.1992/36, K.1993/4 / f) / g) *Resmi Gazete* (Official Gazette), 19.03.1993, 13-32 / h) the Turkish Constitutional Court upheld the 1952 Law on Workers and Employers in the Press Sector which prohibited the publication of newspapers during the first days of two particular religious holidays as a permissible "suspension" of freedom of expression.
91. *McGowan v. Maryland*, 366 US 420 (1961).

which have their day of rest or holy day on a day other than Sunday are adversely affected by the Finnish working-time rules.[92] In contrast, in *R. v. Big M Drug Mart* the Canadian Supreme Court recognised that beyond an allegedly secular surface the Sunday closing rules of the Lord's Day Act had an intrusive nature. Furthermore, Justice Dickson reminded that:

> the guarantee of freedom of conscience prevents the government from compelling individuals to perform or abstain from performing otherwise harmless acts because of the religious significance of those acts to others. The element of religious compulsion is perhaps somewhat more difficult to perceive (especially for those whose beliefs are being enforced) when, as here, it is non-action that is being decreed, but in my view compulsion is nevertheless what it amounts to.[93]

The issue of compulsion (establishment) aside, judicial decisions on Sunday laws are curiously silent about whether such legal rules affect the *forum internum* or – more conveniently – impose a limitation on an external manifestation of religious freedom. It is another striking feature of these cases that most courts are unwilling to consider whether, if at all, the needs of believers whose religion requires them to observe a day other than Sunday as a day of rest should be accommodated. Examples also appear in Strasbourg jurisprudence. In one case the Commission found that the free exercise rights of a Muslim teacher who was not entitled to take time off for Friday prayer were not violated as he accepted the terms of his employment without informing the employer

---

92. *Konttinen v. Finland*, Application No. 24949/94 (1996) 87 DR 68. Note that new Finnish legislation implementing the European working-time directive allows for alternative days of rest.
93. *R. v. Big M Drug Mart Ltd.* [1985] 1 S.C.R. 295, paragraph 133. The difference a court's willingness to see compulsion makes is best illustrated when *Big M* is contrasted with an earlier (pre-Charter) decision of the Canadian Supreme Court where the justices upheld the same law in *R. v. Robertson and Rosetanni*, (1963) S.C.R. 651, paragraph 657. For an analysis of the two decisions, see MacLachlin, B. "Freeedom of Religion and the Rule of Law: A Canadian Perspective", pp. 12-34, in: Farrow, D., ed., *Recognizing Religion in a Secular Society, Essays in Pluralism, Religion, and Public Policy*, McGill-Queens, 2004.

of his religion's requirements to this effect.[94] In yet another case where an evangelical Christian was dismissed after she refused to work on Sundays, the Commission found that she was dismissed not for religious reasons but because she refused to accept the altered contractual terms of her employment.[95] In these decisions the European Commission repeatedly referred to the choice these employees make when signing a contract of employment.[96]

While this stance might be credited for putting due emphasis on individual autonomy (i.e. it was a matter of the employee's personal choice not to inform his employer about his religious conviction), before rushing to a conclusion these decisions shall be seen in the light of further court decisions. In *Prais v. Council*[97] an employee was not able to participate in an employment-related competition because it was scheduled for the day of a Jewish holiday. In rejecting the complaint, the European Court of Justice (ECJ) reportedly emphasised that the applicant did not inform her employer in advance about the upcoming religious holiday which was to prevent her from participating in the competition. In this case, the ECJ said (in para 18) that:

> If it is desirable that an appointing authority informs itself in a general way of dates which might be unsuitable for religious reasons, and seeks to avoid fixing such dates for tests, nevertheless, ... neither the staff regulations nor the fundamental rights already referred to can be considered as imposing on the appointing authority a duty to avoid a conflict with a religious requirement of which the authority has not been informed.

---

94. *X. v. the United Kingdom*, Application No. 8160/78, 22 DR 27. In this case the Commission noted, at 33, however, that "the object of Article 9 is essentially that of protecting the individual against unjustified interference by the State, but that there may also be positive obligations inherent in an effective 'respect' for the individual's freedom of religion." For a discussion of the decisions of domestic courts in the underlying case see Clayton, R. and Tomlinson, H., *The Law of Human Rights*, Oxford, 2000, p. 964.
95. *Steadman v. the United Kingdom*, Application No. 29107/95, 98-A (1997) DR 104.
96. For a critical analysis of commentaries on the European Commission's jurisprudence see Evans, C., *Freedom of Religion*, p. 131.
97. Case 130/75 *Prais v. Council* [1976] ECR 1589.

Although not imposing an obligation on the employer, suggesting that an employer may take measures to accommodate requests stemming from an employee's religious beliefs is at least reassuring. Nonetheless, it is important to remember how forceful the argument about Sunday as a secular day of rest became in national constitutional jurisprudence. The Spanish Constitutional Court rejected the complaint of a Seventh-Day Adventist who was dismissed when she refused to work on Sundays. Although the employee suggested alternative arrangements, Spanish justices emphasised that Sunday was a secular day of rest in Spain and the Court did not even suggest that the employer might have to take measures of accommodation in such cases.[98]

As even a short overview of cases concerning challenges against Sunday closing laws reveals, courts are more willing to admit to superficial arguments about the secular nature of Sunday laws or emphasise the private autonomy of employees in shaping the conditions of their own employment. The issue which courts were avoiding is that of accommodation of the special needs of believers. While such a judicial strategy leaves plenty of room for the political branches to exercise their discretion, it is important to note that, to the extent believers are presenting their requests to private employers, their cases might fall outside the scope of constitutional protection, and their constitutional rights may lack third-party effect in a national legal system. Without due assistance from constitutional courts, lower courts might not be at ease to resolve conflicts between private employers and employees with reference to the employees' religious freedoms or other constitutional considerations. To the extent a constitutional court might be willing to deal with rights of employees in private employment, one also has to be prepared to accept that private employers also may assert constitutional claims. Recently the German Constitutional Court found that "occupational freedom within the meaning of Article 12.1 of the Basic Law protects the employer's interest in employing in his or her business only employees who comply with the employer's expectations, and in restricting the number of employees to the extent that he or she determines." This argument was

---

98. STC 19/1985, 13 February 1985, as described in Martínez-Torrón, J., "Freedom of Religion in the Case Law of the Spanish Constitutional Court", 2001, *Brigham Young University Law Review* 711 (2001).

used to reject a complaint by a woman who had recently converted to Islam and was dismissed for wearing her headscarf to work (Decision GER-2003-3-021 a) Germany / b) Federal Constitutional Court / c) Second Chamber of the First Panel / d) 30-07-2003 / e) 1 BvR 792/03 / f) / g) / h) *Neue Juristische Wochenschrift 2003*, 2815-2816 EuGRZ 2003, 515-517; Codices (German)).

In conclusion, apart from their jurisprudential significance, arguments (or the lack thereof) on coercion and accommodation in Sunday closing cases are worth a closer look as constitutional problems surrounding Sunday closing laws appear to enjoy a strange renaissance in European Union member states in the course of the implementation of Council Directive 93/104/EC of 23 November 1993 concerning certain aspects of the organisation of working time. The directive originally included a provision according to which the weekly day of rest should in principle fall on Sunday (Article 5). The ECJ, however, annulled this requirement, saying that "whilst the question whether to include Sunday in the weekly rest period is ultimately left to the assessment of Member States, having regard, in particular, to the diversity of cultural, ethnic and religious factors in those States ... the fact remains that the Council has failed to explain why Sunday, as a weekly rest day, is more closely connected with the health and safety of workers than any other day of the week."[99] Nonetheless, implementing national legislation retains special provisions for Sundays in several member states. Employers' organisations were also seen to urge their members to circumvent via collective agreements rules making it possible for employees to refuse work on Sunday.[100]

Manifestations of religious freedom: facially neutral limitations and the problem of ritual slaughter

Unlike the *forum internum* which merits no governmental restrictions, external manifestations of religious freedom should withstand limitations under European constitutions and international human rights instruments. In cases before courts, a typical

---

99. C-84/94, *United Kingdom of Great Britain and Northern Ireland v. Council of the European Union* [1996], ECR I-5755, paragraph 37.
100. See, for example, for the Netherlands: "Employers seek to 'circumvent' new Sunday working law through collective agreements", at: http://www.eiro.eurofound.eu.int/2003/01/inbrief/nl0301101n.html.

manifestation of religious exercise appears in the form of believers refusing to follow or openly violating generally applicable legal regulations. Limitations imposed upon freedom of religion are particularly difficult to challenge when they are imposed by facially neutral laws. In such cases, courts are to decide whether the constitutional protection of religious freedom would warrant an exception or exemption benefiting believers.[101] Examples to this effect are abundant; this section will explore cases involving prohibitions on ritual slaughter.

Dietary restrictions are central to numerous faiths and their observance is considered as an important manifestation of religious freedom. While diets are believed to fall within the private sphere, their observance often depends on conforming to such religious rules on slaughter, food preparation and consumption which may contravene general laws on a wide variety of subjects such as public health, animal safety, and may also interfere with regulations on working time and working conditions. Furthermore, dietary regulations stemming from religious requirements might give rise to rights claims in such environments where meals are or need to be offered, i.e. public education, public hospitals, prisons or the armed forces. In multi-religious societies where only a small group of believers follows such dietary regulations, many difficulties are likely to affect believers stemming from (at least prima facie) neutral legal rules.

Believers of religions which require adherence to special diets may suffer from restrictions under generally applicable laws regulating food manufacturing. Although bans on kosher slaughter are known for their anti-Semitic inspiration and historical examples are traumatic, in several European democracies, similar bans exist which are allegedly or at least in part motivated by animal protection considerations.[102] When testing the constitutionality of the limitation imposed by an animal cruelty law on religious freedom the Austrian Constitutional Court held that:

---

101. Problems concerning the wearing of religious symbols or insignia are discussed in detail in the context of religious education in Chapter 2.
102. Note that the European Convention for the Protection of Animals for Slaughter, of 10 May 1979, allows for a specific exemption in order to facilitate ritual slaughter in its Article 17.

Although today the prevention of cruelty to animals is widely recognised as an important public interest its value cannot exceed the right to free exercise of religion. "Public morals" signify just those general ideas of people regarding "correct" conduct of life which are explicitly protected by legal regulation. Kosher butchering is not within the ambit of "public morals" and cannot contradict them (Decision AUT-1998-3-010 a) Austria / b) Constitutional Court / c) / d) 17-12-1998 / e) B 3028/97 / f) / g) to be published in *Erkenntnisse und Beschlüsse des Verfassungsgerichtshofes* (Official Digest) / h) Codices (German)).[103]

As such exemptions are typically granted in relation to a particular religion, further constitutional problems may arise when authorities or courts decide to allow kosher slaughter, but refuse or omit to exempt halal butchering from animal cruelty laws, as the differential treatment amounts to discrimination on grounds of religious belief between Jews and Muslims. The peril was duly recognised by the German Constitutional Court when in 2002 it ruled in favour of a Muslim butcher's claim for an exception to legal rules on animal slaughter. Interestingly, the case was decided not only on grounds of religious freedom but with special emphasis on the pious Muslim butcher's occupational freedom.[104]

Note that although knowledgeable about the fact that many European countries impose restrictions on Jewish and Muslim ritual slaughter (rules which clearly interfere with believers' religious freedom),[105] the ECtHR is not particularly sympathetic about dietary restrictions prescribed by religious doctrine. In *Chaa're Shalom ve Tsedek v. France* the ECtHR – agreeing with the government's

---

103. As a follow-up measure, a new federal law was passed to accommodate religious slaughtering requirements via Austrian federal animal protection regulation (Section 32 of the new Federal Animal Protection Act (*Tierschutzgesetz*), Federal Law Gazette (BGBl) I, No 118/2004). Reported in "EU Network of Independent Experts on Fundamental Rights, Report on the Situation of Fundamental Rights in Austria in 2004" submitted to the network by Manfred Nowak and Alexander Lubich on 3 January 2005, p. 37, available at: http://www.cridho.cpdr.ucl.ac.be/DownloadRep/Reports2004/nacionales/CFR-CDF.repAUSTRIA.2004.pdf
104. BVerfGE 104, 337.
105. *Chaa're Shalom ve Tsedek v. France*, Application No. 27417/95, judgment of 27 June 2000, paragraph 20.

submission – was supportive of the claims of a Jewish religious organisation contesting hindrances which prevented "glatt" kosher slaughter in France, submitting that as long as such meat could be obtained from Belgium, there was no violation of the religious freedom.[106] The reasoning of the ECtHR matches the logic of the Swiss animal protection law which allows for a narrow exception for the importation of kosher and halal meat for the members of Jewish and Muslim religious communities.[107]

It is true that the ECtHR was willing to discuss the facts of the case in meticulous detail concerning the availability of various forms of kosher meat in France. Considering, however, the unwillingness of several European countries to allow exceptions for ritual slaughter, it is disturbing that the ECtHR set its standards so low and decided to provide so little guidance that would be useful beyond the facts of the case. As the Austrian and German cases demonstrate, national constitutional courts tend to be more willing to provide constitutional protection to religious freedom than the ECtHR. It is worth noting, however, that – as the German example suggests – the constitutional protection of freedom of religion is not the only ground which could be successfully invoked against restrictions on ritual slaughter.

While it is impossible to prescribe a generally applicable recipe preventing such restrictions on religious freedom, in conclusion it is worth considering a rule of thumb offered in the Krishnaswami study in the following terms:

> Although it would not seem possible to impose upon the public authorities a duty of securing by positive measures the observance of dietary practices of all faiths in all circumstances, the general rule should be that no one should be prevented from observing the dietary practices prescribed by his religion or belief. In the case of a country which has an economic system under which the Government controls the means of production and distribution, this rule would imply that its public authorities are under an obligation to

---

106. *Chaa're Shalom ve Tsedek v. France*, paragraph 65.
107. Article 9.1, Loi fédérale sur la protection des animaux (LPA) du 9 mars 1978, as amended by Loi fédérale sur la protection des animaux (LPA). Modification du 20 juin 2003 (RO 2003 4181 4182; FF 2002 4395).

place the object necessary for observing dietary practices prescribed by particular faiths, or the means of producing them, at the disposal of members of those faiths.

Note that the approach followed by the ECtHR in *Chaa're Shalom ve Tsedek v. France* is not at odds with this expectation.[108]

Manifestations of religious freedom: refusing blood transfusion on grounds of conscience[109]

A most controversial manifestation of freedom of religion is the refusal of life saving medical treatment (typically blood transfusion) on grounds of conscience. In such cases the manifestation of religious freedom clashes with the interest of the state in safeguarding human life. This public interest seems to be less compelling when one's own life is at risk as a result of a well-considered decision to refuse such treatment, while the state's interest in protecting human life intensifies if the decision affects another's life (may that be a spouse, or a child).[110]

The German Constitutional Court acknowledged such a manifestation of religious freedom saying that:

> The fundamental right to religious freedom enshrined in Article 4 of the Basic Law also protects a person's right to choose to react in the way they deem to be most appropriate to overcome a specific situation in life in accordance with their religious convictions, even if these convictions leave a choice of action.
>
> Even though Article 4 of the Basic Law does not provide for the restriction of the right to religious freedom by the legislator, this right is not unlimited. Such limits have to be based in the constitution itself and must respect the fundamental principle of human dignity guaranteed in Article 1.1 of the Basic Law. Therefore, the freedom of religion has a radiating

---

108. See, for example, Taylor, *Freedom of Religion*, p. 258.
109. For further discussion see also Section 4.2.
110. In addition to protecting human life, the state may also express an interest in protecting the integrity of its healthcare system and the medical profession – arguments which are familiar from cases concerning the right to refuse life saving or life-sustaining treatment.

effect in criminal law, restricting the possibility of the state to punish a person for actions which flow from religious convictions (Decision GER-1971-R-002 a) Germany / b) Federal Constitutional Court / c) First Panel / d) 19-10-1971 / e) 1 BvR 387/65 / f) / g) *Entscheidungen des Bundesverfassungsgerichts* (Official Digest), 32, 98, 266 / h)).

Thereupon the German Constitutional Court found that the conviction of a husband for failing to provide assistance after his wife's death due to her refusal of a blood transfusion during child birth on grounds of conscience, violated the Constitution.[111]

The limits of the government's duty to accommodate claims related to free religious exercise in the form of refusing medical treatment were highlighted by the decision of the Spanish Constitutional Tribunal. In this case, the applicant, a Jehovah's Witness who refused medical treatment requiring blood transfusion in a public hospital, requested the reimbursement of the costs of an alternative treatment not requiring blood transfusion which he underwent in a private hospital. In this case, the Constitutional Tribunal construed the right to refuse medical treatment on grounds of conscience as a purely negative right and said that "the duty of the state to ensure the genuine and effective operation of the right to freedom of religion did not entail any obligation to provide services of another kind for adherents of a given faith so that they might fulfil the requirements of religious observance" (Decision ESP-1996-3-026 a) Spain / b) Constitutional Court / c) Second Chamber / d) 28-10-1996 / e) 166/1996 / f) / g) *Boletín oficial del Estado* (Official Gazette), 291, 03.12.1996, 14-19 / h)).

Decisions concerning the limits of permissible manifestations of religious freedom are even more difficult if the treatment of a child is refused by a religious parent. Such was the case in *B. v. Children's Aid Society of Metropolitan Toronto*, where Justice La Forest, writing for a narrow majority of the Canadian Supreme Court explained that instead of construing the Charter's provision protecting freedom of religion (s.2.(b)) to the effect of including

---

111. Both husband and wife were members of the Association of Evangelical Brotherhood. Refusal of blood transfusion was not among the teachings of the religious organisation, but a matter of the couple's individual conviction. See the relevant excerpt from the case above.

in free exercise the right of parents to refuse medical treatment for their children, such a claim shall be assessed in the course of analysing whether government intervention on behalf of the child would amount to an unjustifiable limitation on the parents' right to free religious exercise.[112] This approach allowed him to find that in this case, the state's interest in protecting children at risk prevailed over the parents' religious freedom.

The *OSCE-Venice Commission Guidelines for review of legislation pertaining to religion or belief* summarise applicable principles in the following terms:

> While many States allow adults to make decisions whether or not to accept certain types of procedures, States typically require that some medical procedures be performed on children despite parental wishes. To the extent that the State chooses to override parental preferences for what the State identifies as a compelling need, and that States legitimately may choose to do so, the laws should nevertheless be drafted in ways that are respectful of those who have moral objections to medical procedures, even if the law does not grant the exemption that is sought.[113]

2.3. Proselytism

As John Witte, Jr. remarked, the "problem of proselytism is one of the great ironies of the democratic revolution of the modern world."[114] While there is no settled definition of the term itself, it is often used in a negative sense.[115] When used in a neutral setting proselytism refers to an act of confessing and communicating one's religious beliefs, and as such is in close connection with

---

112. *B. v. Children's Aid Society of Metropolitan Toronto* (1995) 1 S.C.R. 315, paragraph 383 et seq.
113. *OSCE-Venice Commission Guidelines for review of legislation pertaining to religion or belief*, p. 23, available at: http://www.osce.org/publications/odihr/2004/09/12361_142_en.pdf.
114. Witte, J., Jr., "A Primer on the Rights and Wrongs of Proselytism", 31, *Cumberland Law Review*, 619, 2000-01, p. 619.
115. For a prime example see "The Challenge of Proselytism and the Calling to Common Witness" by the World Council of Churches which uses the term in a clear negative sense on paragraph 19. Available at: http://www.wcc-coe.org/wcc/what/ecumenical/jwgpr-e.html.

such manifestations of free exercise as dispersing (dissemination) religious teachings, evangelisation and missionary activities. While proselytism, if so defined, is a clear instance of the freedom to manifest religion or belief, it is also an activity which aims at the conversion of another to a faith of the proselytiser's own. As noted by the Krishnaswami study, proselytism as a manifestation of religious freedom may actively interfere with another's freedom of maintaining their own religious beliefs or the liberty to freely choose one, and, ultimately, the freedom from coercion in matters of conscience. Thus, one's religious freedom to manifest religious convictions interferes with another's rights in the *forum internum* which should not withstand any limitations. It is not surprising that courts often face difficulties in seeking to strike a proper balance in cases involving restrictions on proselytism. Among numerous other factors, a lack of proper legal definition of the most basic concepts often deters courts from providing principled guidance on the scope of constitutional protection for this manifestation of free exercise.

> ### *Case law*
>
> - ECH-1993-S-002 a) Council of Europe / b) European Court of Human Rights / c) Chamber / d) 25-05-1993 / e) 3/1992/348/421 / f) *Kokkinakis v. Greece* / g) Vol. 260-A, Series A of the Publications of the Court / h) Codices (English, French).
>
> On 2 March 1986, in the home of the Orthodox Christians Mr and Mrs Kyriakaki, the police arrested Mr and Mrs Kokkinakis, Jehovah's Witnesses. According to findings of fact subsequently made by the national courts, the Kokkinakis couple had engaged in discussions with Mrs Kyriakaki. Mr Kokkinakis allegedly attempted to convert her. Her husband had therefore called the police.
>
> The Kokkinakis were later charged with proselytism, an offence punishable under Section 4 of Law No. 1363/1938. On 20 March 1986, the Lasithi Criminal Court convicted them and sentenced them each to four months' imprisonment, convertible to a pecuniary penalty. On 17 March 1987, the Crete Court of Appeal acquitted Mrs Kokkinakis but upheld her husband's conviction. The Court of Cassation dismissed his appeal on points of law in April 1988.

The main question to be solved by the Court of Human Rights was whether the conviction of Mr Kokkinakis infringed his freedom of thought, conscience and religion as guaranteed by Article 9 of the ECHR.

First of all the Court stressed that freedom of conscience, thought and religion is one of the foundations of a democratic society. Its religious dimension is one of the most vital elements making up the identity of the believers and their conception of life. It is also a precious asset for atheists, agnostics, sceptics and the unconcerned. Religious freedom implied freedom to manifest one's religion, not only in community with others, "in public" and within the circle of persons whose faith one shared, but also "alone", and "in private", including, in principle, also the right to try to convince one's neighbour.

The Court pointed out that the fundamental nature of the rights guaranteed by Article 9, ECHR, was also reflected in the wording of the paragraph providing limitations. Unlike the second paragraphs of Articles 8, 10 and 11, which cover all the rights covered in the first paragraphs of those articles, paragraph 2 of Article 9 refers only to the "right to manifest one's religion or belief".

In the circumstances of the case, the Court held that the sentence passed by the national courts amounted to an interference with the exercise of Mr Kokkinakis' right to freedom to manifest his religion or belief (Article 9.1, ECHR). It had to establish whether such interference was justified according to Article 9.2, ECHR. In the instant case, by condemning proselytism, Section 4 of Law No. 1363/1938, pursued the legitimate aim of protecting the rights and freedoms of others in so far as it was designed to punish improper proselytism – not to be confused with true evangelism.

The Court noted, however, that in their reasoning the Greek courts had not sufficiently specified in what way the applicant had attempted to convince Mrs Kyriakaki by improper means. Consequently, the Court held that it had not been shown that the applicant's conviction was justified by a pressing social need. The applicant's conviction appeared to have been disproportionate to the legitimate aim pursued and consequently not "necessary in a democratic society (...)

for the protection of the rights and freedoms of others". Accordingly, there had been a violation of the applicant's right to freedom of thought, conscience and religion (Article 9, ECHR).

- SUI-1999-3-008 a) Switzerland / b) Federal Court / c) First Public Law Chamber / d) 30-06-1999 / e) 1P.571/1998 / f) *Association "Church of Scientology Basel City" and M. v. Council of State and Grand Council of Basel City Canton* / g) *Arrêts du Tribunal fédéral* (Official Digest), 125 I 369 / h) Codices (German).

The Grand Council (parliament) of Basel City Canton transmitted a motion to the Council of State (government) asking to receive a government bill for a law to protect the public against the aggressive propaganda of the Scientologists. On the basis of the government bill, the Grand Council amplified the cantonal law on petty offences. The new provision prescribes penalties for anyone who uses misleading or dishonest recruitment methods in public places. It further authorises the police to expel offenders from public places when they use unlawful methods, particularly of a misleading or dishonest kind, or where passers-by are unreasonably importuned.

In a public law appeal, Ms M. and the association "Church of Scientology Basel City" asked the Federal Court to set aside the new provision in question. The Federal Court dismissed the appeal on the following grounds.

...

Irrespective of how the impugned provision originated, it is not directed strictly at Church of Scientology followers but generally at any group that seeks to recruit passers-by in public places, and is therefore not contrary to Article 4 of the Federal Constitution.

...

Freedom of conscience and belief includes the possibility of recruiting individuals as members of a religious community.

Since the impugned provision constitutes a limitation of that freedom, a clear legal basis is required. The terms "misleading" and "dishonest" are sufficiently precise to define and restrict interference with religious freedom. The court may

> refer to identical concepts employed by federal and cantonal legislation in other areas.
>
> The provision at issue serves an overriding public interest. Firstly, passers-by are to be guaranteed their own freedom of conscience and belief and protected against dishonest, unlawful methods. The criminal law provision is therefore justified. Secondly, expulsion from public places of persons who recruit others in an unlawful and dishonest fashion is consistent with the general duty of the police to maintain order ...

Commentary

As the German Constitutional Court said in one of its earliest decisions on freedom of conscience under Article 4.2 of the Basic Law, this freedom:

> embraces not only the personal freedom to believe or not to believe (i.e. profess a faith, to keep it secret, to renounce a former belief and uphold another), but also the freedom to worship publicly, to proselytize, and to compete openly with other religions.[116]

Despite such uncompromising words from the German Constitutional Court, as the above excerpts also demonstrate, proselytism is a manifestation of religious freedom which has a most dubious reputation among the rights comprising free exercise. The very term carries a glaze of negative connotations, as if referring to some form of malpractice in evangelisation. In this respect the words of Judge Valticos in his partly dissenting judgment in *Larissis v. Greece*[117] are illustrative:

> any attempt going beyond a mere exchange of views and deliberately calculated to change an individual's religious opinions constitutes a deliberate and, by definition, improper act of proselytism, contrary to "freedom of thought, conscience and religion" as enshrined in Article 9 of the Convention. Such acts of proselytism may take forms that are straightforward

---

116. *Rumpelkammer case*, BVerfGE 24, 236 (1968). Available in English in Kommers, *Constitutional Jurisprudence*, p. 446.
117. *Larissis v. Greece*, Application No. 23372/94, No. 26377/94 and No. 26378/94, judgment of 24 February 1998.

or devious, that may or may not be an abuse of the proselytiser's authority and may be peaceful or – and history has given us many bloodstained examples of this – violent. Attempts at "brainwashing" may be made by flooding or drop by drop, but they are nevertheless, whatever one calls them, attempts to violate individual consciences and must be regarded as incompatible with freedom of opinion, which is a fundamental human right.

Reservations about proselytism may be traced back to such historical experiences which cut across centuries and continents. Proselytism is often associated with the advocacy of conversion via coercion, condemned by John Locke in his *Letter Concerning Toleration* (1688) in the following terms:

> No man by nature is bound unto any particular church or sect, but everyone joins himself voluntarily to that society in which he believes he has found that profession and worship which is truly acceptable to God. The hope of salvation, as it was the only cause of his entrance into that communion, so it can be the only reason of his stay there. ... seeing one man does not violate the right of another by his erroneous opinions and undue manner of worship, nor is his perdition any prejudice to another man's affairs, therefore, the care of each man's salvation belongs only to himself. ... Any one may employ as many exhortations and arguments as he pleases, towards the promoting of another man's salvation. But all force and compulsion are to be forborne. Nothing is to be done imperiously. Nobody is obliged in that matter to yield obedience unto the admonitions or injunctions of another, further than he himself is persuaded. Every man in that has the supreme and absolute authority of judging for himself. And the reason is because nobody else is concerned in it, nor can receive any prejudice from his conduct therein.

Constitutional difficulties arising in cases involving restrictions on proselytism highlight the many vulnerabilities of human rights instruments protecting free exercise. When deciding on the constitutionality of limitations imposed on proselytism, courts have to rely on the most basic concepts concerning freedom of religion, many of which resist attempts at proper legal or judicial definition. Defining conversion or coercion in matters of religion turned out to be a most controversial issue for drafters of such international human rights instruments as the Universal Declaration of Human Rights or the ICCPR.[118] In part, such difficulties are attributable to the fact that while certain religions are strongly opposed to proselytism (some being sceptical about incomers, while others refusing incomers and outgoers alike), evangelisation or the spreading of faith is central to the ways of other religious communities. Thus, when such basic concepts as religion, legitimate manifestations of religious exercise or coercion in matters of conscience are used without due care, courts easily contribute to the perpetuation of problematic governmental interference in matters of conscience.[119]

A prohibition on proselytism was inserted in several European constitutions,[120] among which the Greek one is probably the best known in Europe.[121] In *Kokkinakis v. Greece*, the majority judgment of the ECtHR, quoted above at length, refused to provide a comprehensive legal definition of proselytism for the purpose of Article 9 analysis,[122] nor did it seriously consider whether the blanket criminalisation of proselytism as such was acceptable under the European Convention. The justices instead settled on stating that the aim of the Greek law was legitimate as it meant to protect

---

118. See Lerner, N. "Proselytism, Change of Religion, and International Human Rights", 12, *Emory International Law Review*, 477, 1998, p. 478.
119. Conceptions of coercion used by courts in proselytism cases are worth comparing with decisions dealing with governmental measures which were found to amount to impermissible religious indoctrination on account of imposing religious oath requirements or recognising religious holidays as official days of rest. See S 2.2.
120. See, for example, Azerbaijan Constitution (Article 18.2), Cyprus (Article 18.5). See also the Russian Constitution's free speech clause prohibiting compulsion to express or denounce a conviction (Article 29.3) and the prohibition in the Romanian Constitution on compulsion to embrace a religion (Article 29.1). Note that under common law the promotion of religious beliefs might be prohibited if it constitutes a breach of the peace. See *Redmond-Bate v. DPP* (1999), 7, BCHR 375, in Clayton-Tomlinson, *The Law of Human Rights*, p. 958.
121. Article 13(2), Greek Constitution. Note that since 1844, all Greek constitutions have contained a prohibition on proselytism. Kyriazopoulos, K., "Proselytization in Greece: Criminal Offense vs. Religious Persuasion and Equality", *Journal of Law and Religion*, 2004/05, 149, p. 151.
122. In a subsequent admissibility decision, without providing an abstract definition, the ECtHR said that a teacher wearing a headscarf in a public school has a "proselytising effect". *Dahlab v. Switzerland*, Application No. 42393/98, judgment of 15 February 2001.

the "rights and freedoms of others," and did not enquire into the real purpose of the criminal prohibition (i.e. protection of the prevailing Greek Orthodox religion).[123] It is at least disturbing that the ECtHR in the Kokkinakis case took a narrow stance, finding that Greek courts convicted the applicant without proper evidence.

The deferential stance of the majority judgment is in sharp contrast with the views of Judge Martens, partly in dissent, who gives a rich account on the consequences of governmental interference with manifestations of free exercise. This weakness of the majority decision is only furthered by the distinction between "Christian witness" and "improper" forms of proselytism.[124] Note that while it is already problematic, the majority of the ECtHR identifies "Christian witness" with proper proselytism. As Judge Martens duly points out, prohibition of "improper" proselytism is itself problematic, with special regard to "the rising tide of religious intolerance".[125]

In the narrowest context of the case this is unfortunate, as Greece not only imposes a criminal ban on proselytisation, but also refuses to recognise such religious associations which proselytise and criminalises worshipping religions other than the prevailing religion (Greek Orthodox) without a licence.[126] The decision of the ECtHR in the Kokkinakis case is a prime example of judicial deference resulting in the confirmation of markedly intense limitations of free exercise, which is a departure from international trends and standards.[127] True, the ECtHR's position defines a minimum standard allowing member states to afford a higher level of protection

---

123. *Kokkinakis v. Greece*, paragraph 44. Although in this respect the Kokkinakis judgment attracted intense criticism in scholarly circles, the ECtHR repeated its finding in a subsequent decision in *Larrisis and others v. Greece* (1999) 27 EHRR 329, paragraphs 43-44.
    See, for example, Gunn, J. T., "Adjudicating Rights of Conscience under the European Convention on Human Rights", pp. 305-330, in van der Vyver, J. and Witte, J., Jr. (eds), *Religious Human Rights in Global Perspective, Legal Perspectives*, Martinus Nijhoff, 1996, p. 323.
124. *Kokkinakis v. Greece*, paragraph 48.
125. *Kokkinakis v. Greece*, paragraph 16.
126. Kyriazopoulos, "Proselytization in Greece", p. 161. The restriction on public places of worship was found to violate the European Convention in *Manoussakis and others v. Greece*, Application No. 18748/91, judgment of 26 September 1996. On religious associations see also Section 3.1.
127. See, for example, Taylor, *Freedom of Religion*, pp. 64 et seq.

to human rights in their national legal systems. Still, it is important to keep in mind at the outset that restrictions on proselytism frequently tend to target unpopular instances of free exercise or unpopular religions. Thus, a low European minimum standard exposes particularly vulnerable subjects to potentially legitimate governmental oppression.

In addition to Greece, several European states are known for their strong opposition towards proselytism, among them being the Russian Federation, Bulgaria, and Armenia. Paul Taylor suggests that in these jurisdictions hostility towards proselytising religious communities is best explained once one acknowledges the significance of the state or dominant religion in (re)shaping national identity.[128] In these countries, legislative efforts to suppress proselytism are typically directed at new religious movements, often of foreign origin, which are believed by dominant political forces to endanger the societal positions of the state or dominant church.[129] In this respect, it is worth considering John Witte's call for self-restraint on proselytising religious groups, going so far as suggesting that Article 27 of the ICCPR acknowledging a right of religious minorities to "profess and practise their own religion", could have justified a "moratorium for a few years in places like Russia so that the local religions, even the majority Russian Orthodox Church, had some time to recover from nearly a century of harsh oppression. [Adding that] Article 27 cannot permanently insulate local religious groups from interaction with other religions."[130]

Although new democracies might appear particularly willing to suppress new religious movements' proselytising efforts, attempts

---

128. Taylor, *Freedom of Religion*, p. 65.
129. See Durham, W. C., "Perspectives on Religious Liberty, A Comparative Framework", pp. 1-44, in van der Vyver, J. and Witte, J., Jr., eds, *Religious Human Rights in Global Perspective, Legal Perspectives*, Martinus Nijhoff, 1996, at pp. 4-5.
130. See Witte, J., Jr., "A Dickensian Era of Religious Rights: On Religious Human Rights in Global Perspective", 42, *William and Mary Law Review*, 707, 2001, pp. 764-765.
 Article 27, ICCPR: "In those States in which ethnic, religious or linguistic minorities exist, persons belonging to such minorities shall not be denied the right, in community with the other members of their group, to enjoy their own culture, to profess and practise their own religion, or to use their own language."

to limit the activities of unpopular religious movements are not unprecedented in established democracies either. The Swiss law, upheld in the case excerpted above, is a prime example of indirect, facially neutral restrictions curbing proselytism. The Swiss Federal Court's decision – which is also familiar from Austrian constitutional jurisprudence[131] – is in sharp contrast with the position of the US Supreme Court expressed in a case sustaining a challenge against an anti-littering city ordinance which was enforced solely to prevent Jehovah's Witnesses from handing out pamphlets in public. In *Schneider v. New Jersey* the US Supreme Court per Justice Roberts said that:

> the public convenience in respect of cleanliness of the streets does not justify an exertion of the police power which invades the free communication of information and opinion secured by the Constitution. ... (The ordinance) affects all those, who, like the petitioner, desire to impart information and opinion to citizens at their homes. If it covers the petitioner's activities it equally applies to one who wishes to present his views on political, social or economic questions ... It is not a general ordinance to prohibit trespassing. It bans unlicensed communication of any views or the advocacy of any cause from door to door, and permits canvassing only subject to the power of a police officer to determine, as a censor, what literature may be distributed from house to house and who may distribute it. The applicant must submit to that officer's judgment evidence as to his good character and as to the absence of fraud in the "project" he proposes to promote or the literature he intends to distribute, and must undergo a burdensome and inquisitorial examination, including photographing and fingerprinting. In the end, his liberty to communicate with the residents of the town at their homes depends upon the exercise of the officer's discretion.[132]

---

131. See VfSlg. 3505/1959, mentioned in AUT-1950-R-001 a) Austria / b) Constitutional Court / c) / d) 27-09-1950 / e) B 72/50; B 92/53; G 9,17/55; B 185,186/58; B 112/59; B 39/70 / f) Freedom of religious worship (freedom to manifest one's beliefs and freedom from external constraints) / g) *Erkenntnisse und Beschlüsse des Verfassungsgerichtshofes* (Official Digest), 2002/1950 of 27.09.1950, 2610/1953 of 14.12.1953, 2944/1955 of 19.12.1955, 3505/1959 of 11.03.1959, 3711/1960 of 25.03.1960, 6919/1972 of 08.12.1972 / h).
132. *Schneider v. New Jersey*, 308 US 147 (1939), 163-164.

It is crucial to realise that in *Schneider v. New Jersey* the US Supreme Court evaluated the constitutionality of an anti-littering ordinance prohibiting pamphleting (i.e. proselytism) by Jehovah's Witnesses not as a limitation of free religious exercise, but as a restriction on freedom of expression.[133] In contrast, both the ECtHR and the Swiss Federal Court decided about the proselytism cases under the protection of freedom of religion. While the judicial approach emphasising the speech aspect of proselytism might appear on its face to miss the core of the constitutional problem, it is important to see that focusing on the communication aspect of proselytism liberated the US Supreme Court from the burdens of passing judgment about creeds and their followers. This is an important observation, keeping in mind that the decisions of the European courts to a considerable extent turned on distinguishing respectable forms of religious exercise from unacceptable ones. This is all the more unfortunate as potentially derogatory adjectives describing various aspects of religious exercise undermine a court's (and thus a state's) appearance of neutrality. The German Constitutional Court warned about the dangers of such adjectives appearing in governmental communications about religious movements, warning that "the requirement that the state be neutral in its treatment of religious or philosophical creeds and must, therefore, be undertaken with caution. The state is forbidden from depicting a religious or philosophical group in a defamatory, discriminatory or distorted manner." Nonetheless, the German Constitutional Court had no objections against the government using the terms "cult" and "sect" in the same communication warning the general public about potentially dangerous religious practices (Decision GER-2002-H-001 a) Germany / b) Federal Constitutional Court / c) First Panel / d) 26-06-2002 / e) 1 BvR 670/91 / f) / g) *Entscheidungen des Bundesverfassungsgerichts* (Official Digest), 105, 279-312 / h) *Neue Juristische Wochenschrift*, 2002, 2626-2632; *Europäische Grundrechte Zeitschrift*).

As the above discussion also suggests, courts are not particularly successful about delineating permissible limitations of proselytism in general terms. In Kokkinakis, the ECtHR did not succeed in explaining what the "rights and freedoms of others" need to

---

133. The interaction of freedom of speech and freedom of religion jurisprudence is covered also on account of the prohibition of blasphemy and other forms of expression interfering with religious sensitivities in Section 4.1.

be protected from if proselytism is not coercive.[134] Although not involving an attempt at defining coercion, it is clear from a more recent admissibility decision of the ECtHR that proselytising from the bench of a court of law by a judge amounts to a form of religious exercise which is not worthy of protection under Article 9 of the European Convention.[135]

2.4. Conscientious objection to military service

Conscientious objection to compulsory military service (conscription) is undeniably an important aspect of religious freedom.[136] Nonetheless, both the ICCPR and the ECHR recognise a right to conscientious objection not in the context of freedom of religion,[137] but as a form of forced labour.[138] Furthermore, while the overwhelming majority of Council of Europe member states recognise the rights of conscientious objectors in their legal systems, they do so in the shadow of constitutional provisions which mention military service or national service as a constitutional duty[139] and which do not always make note of conscientious objection to military service in express terms. Thus, the tension between religious freedom and the duty to participate in national defence is well pronounced before any court addressing a claim of conscientious objection to military service.

Depending on their beliefs, some conscientious objectors refuse to undertake any form of military service altogether (total objectors), while others prefer to withdraw only from such duties which

---

134. Taylor, *Freedom of Religion*, p. 72.
135. *Pitkevich v. Russia*, Application No. 47936/99 (inadmissible).
136. Conscientious objection to other legal rules and obligations is not discussed in the following pages.
137. Compare with Article 10.2 of the EU Charter on Fundamental Rights recognising conscientious objection as a right.
138. See ICCPR, Article 8.3.ii, ECHR, Article 4.3.b. Note that the language of Article 4 of the ECHR is limited to conscientious objectors "in countries, where they are recognised". Also, Malta Constitution, Article 35.2.c.
139. Military service is also mentioned in the constitutions of such countries which otherwise do not require compulsory military service. For example, Hungarian Constitution, Article 70/H.1.

require the use of arms.[140] In most European democracies, objectors are typically required to undertake alternative service (civilian, substitute or non-armed service), the duration of which might exceed that of armed service. Total objection to military service, including the refusal of alternative service entails sanctions (typically, criminal punishment). Although among religious objectors Jehovah's Witnesses are best known for refusing military service altogether, among conscientious objectors one also finds non-religious objectors,[141] like pacifists.[142]

Although a growing number of Council of Europe member states opt for abolishing conscription, in an account of religious freedom one cannot skip addressing constitutional problems surrounding conscientious objection, not only for the benefit of potential objectors who still face conscription, but also in order to protect the religious freedom of already conscripted or contracted military personnel who have developed deep convictions against bearing arms while serving in the military. Cases involving conscientious objectors holding non-religious beliefs assist in defining the outer limits of the constitutional protection of the *forum internum* in matters of freedom of conscience.[143]

---

140. The significance of this distinction was stressed by the Supreme Court of the Netherlands in NED-1995-1-005 a) The Netherlands / b) Supreme Court / c) Second Division / d) 18-04-1995 / e) 99.320 / f) / g) / h) *Delikt en Delinkwent*, 95.289; *Nederlandse Jurisprudentie*, 1995, 611. There has been no conscription in the Netherlands since 1996.
141. As reinforced, for example, in CZE-2003-1-005 a) Czech Republic / b) Constitutional Court / c) Plenary / d) 26-03-2003 / e) Pl. ÚS 42/02 / f) Freedom of conscience / g) *Sbrka zákonu* (Official Gazette), No. 106/2003 / h) Codices (Czech). Note that there has been no conscription in the Czech Republic since 2004.
142. NOR-1996-R-002 a) Norway / b) Supreme Court / c) / d) 23-04-1996 / e) Inr 43B/1996 / f) / g) *Norsk Retstidende* (Official Gazette), 1996, 513 / h) Codices (Norwegian).
143. See Ovey, C. and Robin C. A. White, eds, *Jacobs and White, The European Convention on Human Rights*, Oxford, 2006, fourth edition, p. 308.

Case law

- POR-1995-3-011 a) Portugal / b) Constitutional Court / c) Plenary / d) 05-12-1995 / e) 681/95 / f) / g) *Diário da República* (Official Gazette) (Series II), 25, 30.01.1996, 1501-1511 / h) Codices (Portuguese).[144]

The right to conscientious objection, as a corollary of freedom of conscience, takes the form of opposition to general legislation based on individual conscience, because of personal convictions that prevent the individual from respecting that legislation, and extends beyond obligations arising from compulsory military service to other areas.

In the specific area of conscientious objection to military service, the Constitution requires conscientious objectors to undertake civilian service for an equivalent period and of equivalent difficulty to military service.

In the case of conscientious objection, the principle that citizens should bear an equal share of the community burden requires a balance to be struck between freedom of conscience and the right and duty to defend the homeland, such that the harmonisation of these constitutional values safeguards the freedom while not dispensing with the duty. This is why the right to conscientious objection to military service is linked to the requirement to undertake civilian service as an alternative.

Individuals' obligation to declare themselves available for civilian service, thus excluding recognition of a "total objector" status, cannot be deemed an excessive or unreasonable requirement, and is not, therefore, unconstitutional.

- GER-1985-R-001 a) Germany / b) Federal Constitutional Court / c) Second Panel / d) 24-04-1985 / e) 2 BvR 2, 3, 4/83, 2/84 / f) / g) *Entscheidungen des Bundesverfassungsgerichts* (Official Digest), 69, 1 / h) .

---

144. Note that there is no conscription in Portugal since 2004. In 2001, the Portuguese legislature opened the way before total objectors with adopting Article 12.3 of Law No. 16/2001 of 21 June on religious freedom. Available in English at: http://religlaw.org/template.php?id=415#_ftn.

In regulating the right of conscientious objection, the law must respect the fundamental right guaranteed by Article 4.3 of the Basic Law, while taking due account of the Constitution's basic decision in favour of effective national military defence.

The alternative service provided for in Article 12a.2 of the Basic Law is restricted to persons liable for military service who refuse to perform armed military service for reasons of conscience. It follows that the legislator has a duty to ensure that only those persons who can be assumed with reasonable certainty to satisfy the requirements of the first sentence of Article 4.3 of the Basic Law are recognised as conscientious objectors (confirmed by BVerfGE 48, 127). The new Conscientious Objection Regulating Act meets these requirements.

Under the second sentence of Article 12a.2 of the Basic Law, the legally permissible period of military service is the maximum period of alternative service. The purpose of the second sentence of Article 12a.2 of the Basic Law is to ensure that the burden on persons doing military service and persons doing alternative service is the same. In determining the duration of alternative service within the limits set by the second sentence of Article 12a.2 of the Basic Law, the legislator may therefore take account of the differences between military and alternative service.

Conscientious objectors who belong to ideological groups which oppose armed military service on principle, and whose rejection of such service on grounds of conscience thus appears self-evident, are nonetheless obliged, like all others who claim the fundamental right guaranteed by Article 4.3 of the Basic Law, to explain the reasons for their decision. The fundamental right to freedom of religion (Article 4.1 of the Basic Law) does not relieve them of this obligation.

The principles of proportionality and equal treatment (Article 3.1 of the Basic Law), which are grounded in the rule of law, are not violated by the fact that conscientious objectors, regardless of their obligation to perform alternative service, must be recognised as such in administrative proceedings ...

> Under the first sentence of Section 1.6.1 of the Conscientious Objection Regulating Act, the Federal authority may reject an application to be recognised as a conscientious objector only if it concludes with certainty, on the basis of a fully-detailed application, that the applicant's motives do not entitle him to refuse to perform military service.
>
> In recognition proceedings, the authority concerned is not obliged to disprove the applicant's claim that he refuses to perform military service for reasons of conscience – in other words, the authority is not obliged to accept it if there is a doubt.
>
> Under the Basic Law, the second sentence of Section 1.8 of the Conscientious Objection Regulating Act (conscription when the country is threatened with, or under, attack) must be interpreted in such a way that the conscript may, until the recognition proceedings have been finally concluded, be required only to perform unarmed duties. Thus interpreted, this provision does not interfere with the fundamental right protected by the first sentence of Article 4.3 of the Basic Law. It exempts applicants only from activities which, in the current state of weapons technology, are directly connected with the use of weapons of war.

Commentary

International human rights law does not recognise a right to conscientious objection to military service as a manifestation of religious freedom. Nonetheless, conscientious objection is mentioned expressly in a number of European (and predominantly post-communist) constitutions,[145] although an express rule prescribing an opportunity for alternative military service appears therein less frequently.[146] And still, when it comes to recognising or enforcing

---

145. See, for example, Czech Charter of Fundamental Rights and Freedoms (Article 15.3), Estonian Constitution (124.2), German Basic Law (Article 4.3), Netherlands' Constitution (Article 99), Polish Constitution (Article 85.3), Portuguese Constitution (Article 41.6), Romanian Constitution (Article 42.2.a), Russian Constitution (59.3), Slovak Constitution (Article 25.2), Slovene Constitution (Article 46), Ukraine Constitution (Article 35.4).
146. See Croatian Constitution (Article 47), German Basic Law (Article 12a.2), Hungarian Constitution (Article 70/H) and Russian Constitution (59.3).

the right of conscientious objectors, national courts often appear reserved or perplexed. A good source of examples in this respect is Spanish constitutional jurisprudence.[147] The Spanish Constitution expressly recognises the right to conscientious objection to military service (Article 30.2). In 1982, the Spanish Constitution said that conscientious objection is "a right recognised explicitly and implicitly in the Spanish constitutional order" as an aspect of freedom of ideology protected by the Spanish Constitution (Article 16).[148] Then, with a departure from this stance, in 1987, Spanish constitutional justices famously said that a right to conscientious objection to military service is "a constitutional right which is autonomous but not fundamental." The Court said that a general right to conscientious objection cannot be derived from freedom of conscience as it "would imply denying the very idea of State." The only solution is that conscientious objection "is exceptionally admitted with regard to a particular duty."[149] Subsequently, in 1994, the Constitutional Court then said that "the right to be exempted from military service does not directly follow from the exercise of the right to freedom of ideology but only from the fact that the Constitution expressly recognises the right to conscientious objection, which only applies to military service. The exercise of this right implies recognition of the duty to perform substitute community service" (Decision ESP-1994-3-038 a) Spain / b) Constitutional Court / c) First Chamber / d) 28-11-1994 / e) 321/1994 / f) / g) *Boletín oficial del Estado* (Official Gazette), 310, 57, 28.12.1994 / h)).[150] According to Javier Martínez-Torrón, the indecision of the Spanish Constitutional Court may be attributed to the fact that – in addition to recognising freedom of conscience (Article 16) and the right

---

147. There has been no conscription in Spain since 2001. The account of Spanish jurisprudence follows Martínez-Torrón, Case Law of the Spanish Constitutional Court. All English-language excerpts are from this source, unless marked otherwise.
148. 15/1982, 23 April 1982, FJ 6.
149. STC 161/1987, 27 October 1987, FJ 3. In the case the Spanish Constitutional Court reviewed legislation on conscientious objection which was passed in 1984.
150. For a similar position see ARG-1989-R-001 a) Argentina / b) Supreme Court of Justice of the Nation / c) / d) 18-04-1989 / e) / f) Portillo, Alfredo s/infr. art. 44 ley 17.531 / g) *Fallos de la Corte Suprema de Justicia de la Nación* (Official Digest), 312, 496 / h) Codices (Spanish).

to conscientious objection to military service (Article 30.2) – the Spanish Constitution makes military service a "constitutional right and duty" in express terms (Article 30.1).[151] The difficulties of a similar balancing exercise are sensed in many constitutional court decisions in this field. Still, note that where the constitution does not recognise conscientious objection expressly, courts may still be ready to accept it as an aspect of free exercise but as a statutory right, as did the Austrian Constitutional Court in AUT-1927-R-002 a) Austria / b) Constitutional Court / c) / d) 16-05-1927 / e) B 442/26 et al.; B 399, 437/26; B 392, 438/26; B 41/31; B 229/56; B 146/58; B 122/67; B 13/68; B 205/74; B 213/74; B 55/76; B 248/75; B 438/84; B 714/83; B 460/86; B 1044/86 / f) Freedom of conscience (freedom of self-determination in relation to acts reflecting personal beliefs, including religious beliefs) / g) *Erkenntnisse und Beschlüsse des Verfassungsgerichtshofes* (Official Digest), 799/1927, 800/1927, 802/1927 of 16.05.1927, 1408/1931 of 23.06.1931, 3220/1957 of 28.06.1957, 3480/1958 of 17.12.1958, 5583/1967 of 09.10.1967, 5809/1968 of 15.10.1968, 7494/1975 of 06.03.1975, 7679/1975 of 28.11.1975, 7907/1976 of 15.10.1976, 8033/1977 of 26.03.1977, 10.674/1985 of 23.11.1985, 10.915/ 1986 of 19.06.1986, 11.105/1986 of 28.11.1986, 11.253/1987 of 02.03.1987 / h).

Court decisions concerning the rights of conscientious objectors exhibit interesting instances of judicial balancing involving the protection of religious freedom (and other constitutional rights associated with it) on the one hand, and constitutional duties and the demands of national security and national defence on the other. As a rule, the more serious weight is attributed to national security interests, the less room is left for free exercise. In such cases, much depends on courts' own preferences. For instance, while the Croatian Constitutional Court found that imposing a deadline within which a conscript has to indicate an objection violates "the freedom to change one's conviction,"[152] the Slovakian Constitutional Court approved such a deadline, holding that the military's need to know the number of service persons for their

---

151. Martínez-Torrón, Case Law of the Spanish Constitutional Court, note 135.
152. CRO-1998-1-004 a) Croatia / b) Constitutional Court / c) / d) 18-02-1998 / e) U-I-20/1992 / f) / g) *Narodne novine* (Official Gazette), 31/1998, pp. 697-699 / h) Codices (Croatian, English).

proper operation prevailed over freedom of religion.¹⁵³ It seems that in contexts where public peace might depend on the instant availability of military force, courts are likely to defer to the assessment of military authorities in matters of conscientious objectors (Decision CYP-2001-2-002 a) Cyprus / b) Supreme Court / c) / d) 04-11-1983 / e) 4408, 4411 / f) *Pitsillides and Another v. Republic* / g) Cyprus Law Reports (1983) 2 C.L.R. 374 (Official Digest) / h)).

Arguments about the nature of the constitutional duty to serve one's country are often presented using an equality rhetoric which is not sensitive to issues of conscience.¹⁵⁴ A similar argument was also introduced by the High Court of Israel, where the justices said that in the case of conscientious objectors, freedom of religion should be balanced against:

> the injustice in exempting part of the population from a general duty imposed on all, especially since this duty entails risking one's life and as the exemption might jeopardise national security, result in unjust administrative effects and discrimination ... In a society as pluralistic as Israel, the recognition of selective conscientious objection might loosen the links that hold us together as a people and turn the people's army into an army of peoples, made up of different units, each having its own spheres in which it can act conscientiously, and others in which it cannot. The Court noted that in a polarised society this consideration carries considerable weight (Decision ISR-2002-3-005 a) Israel / b) High Court of Justice / c) Panel

---

153. As summed up in SVK-1995-2-005 a) Slovakia / b) Constitutional Court / c) Plenary / d) 24-05-1995 / e) PL. US 18/95 / f) Case of unconstitutional restriction of religious faith in relationship to the military service / g) *Zbierka nálezov a uznesen Ústavného súdu Slovenskej republiky* (Official Digest), 1995, pp. 171-189 / h) Codices (Slovak). For a similar position see also CZE-1999-1-007 a) Czech Republic / b) Constitutional Court / c) / d) 02-06-1999 / e) Pl. US 18/98 / f) / g) / h) Codices (Czech).
Note that there has been no conscription in Slovakia since 2005.
154. The Czech Constitutional Court used the equality rationale to reject a claim for complete exemption from military service on grounds of conscience. CZE-1995-3-010 a) Czech Republic / b) Constitutional Court / c) Fourth Chamber / d) 18-09-1995 / e) IV. US 81/95 / f) Conscientious Objectors and the Duty to Perform National Service / g) 4 *Sbrka zákonu* (Official Gazette), 50 / h) Codices.

/ d) 30-12-2002 / e) H.C. 7622/02 / f) *Zonenstein v. The Chief Military Advocate* / g) not yet published / h)).

Equality concerns are intense in jurisdictions which exempt followers or priests of particular religions from military service, while staying silent about others. Although such statutory exemptions seem to depart on their face from requirements of non-discrimination and state neutrality in matters of faith, initially the European Commission on Human Rights refused to find that such unequal treatment of believers amounted to discrimination under the Convention.[155] Recently, however, the ECtHR declared admissible a challenge[156] against the Austrian alternative service law which allows an exemption for ministers of "recognised religious societies."[157] The applicants are Jehovah's Witnesses who are not covered by the statutory exemption.[158]

Among individuals who do not qualify for a statutory exemption, those who belong to a religious community which is known to refuse armed service may enjoy a de facto advantage over others who hold personal convictions to the same effect. This conclusion may be derived from a decision of the European Commission in a case[159] concerning a Swedish pacifist who applied as a conscientious

---

155. See, for example, *Grandrath v. Federal Republic of Germany*, Application No. 2299/64, 1967 YB 626.
Although in one case the Commission seems to have adopted a more stringent standard which does not tolerate such a distinction between religious ministers, the decision of the ECtHR in the same case did not touch upon this issue. See *Tsirlis and Kouloumpas v. Greece*, Application No.19233/91; No. 19234/91, judgment of 29 May 1997.
156. *Gütl v. Austria*, Application No. 49686/99 (admissibility decision of 1 February 2005).
157. Civilian Service Act (*Zivildienstgesetz*), Section 13a.1.
158. Furthermore, Section 11.1 of the Federal Act on the Legal Status of Registered Religious Communities (*Bundesgesetz über die Rechtspersönlichkeit von religiösen Bekenntnisgemeinschaften*, hereafter referred to as the "1998 Act"), which had entered into force on 10 January 1998, established that recognition under the Recognition Act was only possible after 10 years' existence as a registered religious community, thus effectively postponing the effective date of the recognition to 2008.
159. *N. v. Sweden*, Application No. 10410/83 (1985), 40 DR 203.

objector seeking the same treatment to which Jehovah's Witnesses were subjected.[160] In this case, the Commission said that:

> membership of such a religious sect as Jehovah's Witnesses is an objective fact which creates a high degree of probability that exemption is not granted to persons who simply wish to escape service, since it is unlikely that a person would join such a sect only for the purpose of not having to perform military or substitute service. The same high probability would not exist if exemption was also granted to individuals claiming to have objections of conscience to such service or to members of various pacifist groups or organisations.[161]

Note that the position of the European Commission is not in harmony with the position of General Comment No. 22 saying that "there shall be no differentiation among conscientious objectors on the basis of the nature of their particular beliefs."[162]

It would be simplistic to read the requirement of membership to a religious community which is known to object to military service as a sign of establishment of religion. Rather, one must see it as an unfortunate outcome of a search for a trustworthy indicator of the seriousness of one's convictions. Indeed, determining the sincerity of beliefs is a central problem in cases involving conscientious objectors. On the role of courts in testing the sincerity of beliefs, the Justice Iacobucci, writing for the majority of the Canadian Supreme Court in *Syndicat Northcrest v. Amselem*, said the following:

> Assessment of sincerity is a question of fact that can be based on several non-exhaustive criteria, including the credibility of a claimant's testimony, as well as an analysis of whether the alleged belief is consistent with his or her other current religious practices. It is important to underscore, however, that it is inappropriate for courts rigorously to study and focus on the past practices of claimants in order to determine whether their current beliefs are sincerely held. Over the course of a

---

160. Jehovah's Witnesses received total objector status under Article 46 of the Swedish Conscript Act. The relevant provision of the Conscript Act is reproduced in English, idem, p. 205.
161. *N. v. Sweden*, p. 208.
162. *General Comment No. 22*, p. 11.

lifetime, individuals change and so can their beliefs. Religious beliefs, by their very nature, are fluid and rarely static. A person's connection to or relationship with the divine or with the subject or object of his or her spiritual faith, or his or her perceptions of religious obligation emanating from such a relationship, may well change and evolve over time. Because of the vacillating nature of religious belief, a court's enquiry into sincerity, if anything, should focus not on past practice or past belief but on a person's belief at the time of the alleged interference with his or her religious freedom.[163]

The Croatian Constitutional Court invalidated the law which allowed the Ministry of Justice to re-examine one's eligibility for alternative service if the person exhibited slovenly conduct and violated disciplinary rules during his time of civilian service (Decision CRO-1998-1-004 a) Croatia / b) Constitutional Court / c) / d) 18-02-1998 / e) U-I-20/1992 / f) / g) *Narodne novine* (Official Gazette), 31/1998, 697-699 / h) Codices (Croatian, English)).

As was already indicated, ascertaining the sincerity of beliefs is especially problematic in the case of such conscientious objectors who refer to non-religious grounds (e.g. pacifists).[164] In this respect, the Supreme Court of Norway said that "the conscript must have a fundamentally pacifist attitude. This attitude must imply something more than the mere fact that it appears wrong to the conscript himself personally to perform military service. If this condition is not met, the conscript's conviction can only be considered an individual, subjective norm, without basis in a system of rules with more universal validity" (Decision NOR-1996-R-001 a) Norway / b) Supreme Court / c) / d) 23-04-1996 / e) Inr 42B/1996 / f) / g) *Norsk Retstidende* (Official Gazette), 1996, 509 / h) Codices (Norwegian)).[165] As de

---

163. *Syndicat Northcrest v. Amselem* [2004] 2 S.C.R. 551, 2004 SCC 47, paragraphs 52-53.

164. See, for example, HUN-1994-3-015 a) Hungary / b) Constitutional Court / c) / d) 21-10-1994 / e) 46/1994 / f) / g) *Magyar Közlöny* (Official Gazette), 103/1994 / h): The Court found unconstitutional a provision of the government decree which excluded those persons who possessed firearms during the year before they declared their objection from the possibility of alternative service.

165. On this, see CRO-1998-1-004 a) Croatia / b) Constitutional Court / c) / d) 18-02-1998 / e) U-I-20/1992 / f) / g) *Narodne novine* (Official Gazette), 31/1998, pp. 697-699 / h) Codices (Croatian, English).

Sousa e Brito notes, in most countries, "the law of conscientious objection admits ethical objection only if it pertains to all kinds of war, but not merely objection to a particular war or to certain kinds of weapons."[166]

Questions about the sincerity of one's beliefs against military service have an even longer shadow, once claims from partial and total objectors are weighed. The paradox of testing the sincerity of beliefs of partial and total objectors was pointed out by the Israeli High Court, when it noted that "the weight of the considerations against the recognition of conscientious objection is much heavier in selective conscientious objection than in 'complete' conscientious objection" (Decision ISR-2002-3-005 a) Israel / b) High Court of Justice / c) Panel / d) 30-12-2002 / e) H.C. 7622/02 / f) *Zonenstein v. The Chief Military Advocate* / g) not yet published / h)). "Total objectors" who are unwilling to submit to alternative (unarmed) service face sanctions, typically criminal punishment, for their refusal. In order to prevent such convictions in Germany, it has become a practice not to draft believers who would refuse to undertake military service altogether.[167]

Conscientious objectors who are willing to perform some sort of substitute duties are typically accommodated via unarmed alternative (substitute or civil) service. It is not unusual for the duration of such alternative service to exceed the length of armed service. The German Basic Law, for instance, expressly provides that the period of alternative service shall not exceed that of military service (Article 12a(2)). When the Christian Democrat government expanded the length of alternative service so as it became five months longer than armed military service, the Constitutional Court found this extension constitutional, noting that with the extension, alternative service has become as long as military training together with reserve duty.[168] According to the practice of the

---

166. de Sousa e Brito, J. "Conscientious Objection", pp. 273-290, in Lindholm, T., Durham, W. C., Jr., and Tahzib-Lie, B. G., eds., *Facilitating Freedom of Religion or Belief: A Deskbook*, Martinus Nijhoff, 2004, p. 279 (also citing examples to the contrary on pp. 278-279).
167. Robbers, G., "The Permissible Scope of Legal Limitations on the Freedom of Religion or Belief in Germany", 17, *Emory International Law Review*, 841, 2005, p. 864.
168. BVerfGE 69, 1.

UN Human Rights Committee, the length of alternative service cannot be set in a manner so as to test the sincerity of beliefs of individuals' convictions,[169] nor can the length of alternative service be punitive. Greece has been repeatedly warned by international human rights protectors about its alternative service being disproportionately long.[170] Although the length of military service was reduced by a new law in 2005, currently Greek armed service still remains at 12 months, while alternative service shall be a minimum of 23 months.[171]

Although alternative service in many countries is performed outside the confines of military establishment, the Austrian Constitutional Court found that contracting out to a private institution (the Red Cross in this particular case) the management of alternative service altogether was also unconstitutional. According to Austrian constitutional jurisprudence, alternative service is still a duty performed towards the state, therefore the state remains under an obligation to ensure that fundamental rights of conscripts are not violated during their alternative service.[172]

Procedures of filing a request for alternative service and the process of its evaluation affect the core of the exercise of the right,

---

169. *Frederic Foin v. France*, Communication No. 666/1995 (views of 3 November 1999), (2000) 7(2) IHRR 354. On this issue see Taylor, *Freedom of Religion*, p. 194.
170. See European Committee of Social Rights: Complaint No. 8/2000, Quaker Council for European Affairs (QCEA) against Greece and also the follow-up Council of Europe Committee of Ministers' Resolution ResChS(2002)3. Also, concluding observations of the UN Human Rights Committee: Greece. 25/04/2005, CCPR/CO/83/GRC.
171. As reported by Amnesty International in "Greece: High time to comply fully with European standards on conscientious objection", 1 May 2006, at: http://news.amnesty.org/library/Index/ENGEUR250032006?open&of=ENG-GRC. The length of alternative service significantly exceeds that of armed service in Estonia, Finland and Latvia.
172. Article 54a of the Civil Service Act. Reported in "Report on the situation of fundamental rights in Austria in 2004", p. 38.

and therefore are crucial for its meaningful exercise.[173] An important procedural issue is the time-frame within which a conscript has to file a request. From jurisprudence it appears that while too short time-limits around conscription might present a problem, a real issue is whether a request might be filed during military service. After all, missing the deadline in such cases results in a permanent forfeiture of this aspect of freedom of religious exercise.[174] Constitutional courts seem to prefer solutions which permit individuals in military service to manifest their convictions not only before, but also during their terms of service. Such a judicial stance allows for contracted military personnel to adjust the terms of their service to a change in their beliefs, should the need arise. Note that depriving active servicemen from such an opportunity would violate requirements of equal treatment.[175] The Polish Constitutional Court was also willing to acknowledge a right of professional servicemen to be discharged from service on grounds of conscientious objection (Decision POL-1999-1-003 a) Poland / b) Constitutional Tribunal / c) / d) 16-02-1999 / e) SK 11/98 / f) / g) *Dziennik Ustaw Rzeczypospolitej Polskiej* (Official Gazette), 10.03.1999, item 182; *Orzecznictwo Trybunalu Konstytucyjnego Zbiór Urzedowy* (Official Digest), 1998, No. 2 / h) Codices (English, Polish)).

Although constitutional courts tend not to raise objections against legal regimes which impose criminal punishment on conscripts

---

173. Note that procedural guarantees for the treatment of conscientious objectors may well be developed in cases which do not involve religious freedom issues. See *De Jong, Baljet and van den Brink v. the Netherlands*, 8805/79; 8806/79; 9242/81, judgment of 22 May 1984 where the ECtHR enforced the right of prompt access to a judicial officer (Article 5.3, ECHR) for conscientious objectors held in custody until a decision is made in their case.
174. CZE-1999-1-007 a) Czech Republic / b) Constitutional Court / c) / d) 02-06-1999 / e) Pl. US 18/98 / f) / g) / h) Codices (Czech), CRO-1998-1-004 a) Croatia / b) Constitutional Court / c) / d) 18-02-1998 / e) U-I-20/1992 / f) / g) *Narodne novine* (Official Gazette), 31/1998, 697-699 / h) Codices (Croatian, English).
175. See CRO-1998-1-004 a) Croatia / b) Constitutional Court / c) / d) 18-02-1998 / e) U-I-20/1992 / f) / g) *Narodne novine* (Official Gazette), 31/1998, 697-699 / h) Codices (Croatian, English).

refusing military service,[176] criminal sanctions imposed upon conscientious objectors appear to invite considerable litigation. To begin with, once conscripted, applicants awaiting a final decision on their conscientious objector status who refuse military service might face criminal sanctions for insubordination.[177] In order to prevent such convictions, the German Constitutional Court ruled that during this initial period conscripts filing for alternative service may only be assigned to unarmed service.[178] Constitutional challenges are also often directed at the kind and length of proper sentences in such cases.[179]

"Total objectors", however, face more serious burdens, ultimately even in the form of chain convictions, a solution which both national constitutional courts[180] and recently the ECtHR found

---

176. See, for example, ESP-1996-1-010 a) Spain / b) Constitutional Court / c) Plenary / d) 28-03-1996 / e) 55/1996 / f) / g) Boletín oficial del Estado (Official Gazette), 102, 27.04.1996, 48-59 / h). ("Neither the organisation of, nor services related to, the alternative community service – civil defence, environmental work, social and public health services, etc. – inherently implied the performance of activities which could impinge upon the personal convictions of any person who objected to military service..."). For a similar view from the German Constitutional Court, see BVerfGE 19, 135 and BVerfGE 24, 178. Also GER-1970-R-001 a) Germany / b) Federal Constitutional Court / c) First Panel / d) 26-05-1970 / e) 1 BvR 83/69, 1 BvR 244/69, 1 BvR 345/69 / f) / g) *Entscheidungen des Bundesverfassungsgerichts* (Official Digest), 28, 243 / h) and HUN-1994-3-015 a) Hungary / b) Constitutional Court / c) / d) 21-10-1994 / e) 46/1994 / f) / g) *Magyar Közlöny* (Official Gazette), 103/1994 / h).

177. As the Supreme Court said in another case: "if the conscript accepted the use of armed forces in UN-operations, he should not be considered as having such a serious conviction as is required by the act of exemption from military service, due to reasons of conscientious objection." NOR-1996-R-002 a) Norway / b) Supreme Court / c) / d) 23-04-1996 / e) Inr 43B/1996 / f) / g) *Norsk Retstidende* (Official Gazette), 1996, p. 513 / h) Codices (Norwegian).

178. The German Constitutional Court found this solution constitutional in GER-1970-R-001 a) Germany / b) Federal Constitutional Court / c) First Panel / d) 26-05-1970 / e) 1 BvR 83/69, 1 BvR 244/69, 1 BvR 345/69 / f) / g) *Entscheidungen des Bundesverfassungsgerichts* (Official Digest), 28, 243 / h).

179. Above, GER-1985-R-001 a) Germany / b) Federal Constitutional Court / c) Second Panel / d) 24-04-1985 / e) 2 BvR 2, 3, 4/83, 2/84 / f) / g) *Entscheidungen des Bundesverfassungsgerichts* (Official Digest), 69, 1 / h) .

180. On Germany see Kommers, p. 459. See also DEN-1995-R-001va) Denmark / b) Supreme Court / c) / d) 08-08-1995 / e) II 449/1994 / f) / g) / h) *Ugeskrift for Retsvæsen*, 1995, 828; Codices (Danish).

impermissible.¹⁸¹ In this respect, the Italian Constitutional Court noted that "while it appears plausible that, for an objector, serving a sentence may represent the price paid for breach of a constitutionally stipulated duty, on the other hand regulations can appear at odds with the constitutional protection secured to rights of conscience if they allow penalties to be re-imposed in the event of persistent refusal and thereby exert moral pressure over the objector which, being apt to make him alter elements of his conscience, offends against the recognition by the Constitution of the individual's autonomy over his conscience" (Decision ITA-1997-R-001 a) Italy / b) Constitutional Court / c) / d) 10-02-1997 / e) 43/1997 / f) / g) *Gazzetta Ufficiale, Prima Serie Speciale* (Official Gazette), 9, 26.02.1997 / h) Codices (Italian)). Lastly, it is important to remember that in its jurisprudence, the ECtHR reinforced the Convention's procedural safeguards in cases involving conscientious objectors.¹⁸²

Conscientious objectors may face inconvenient legal consequences for manifesting their religious convictions beyond the context of military service. Objectors who were subjected to criminal sanctions for their refusal to serve in the military do not have a clean criminal record. Under Greek law, only such persons could become chartered accountants, who – among meeting other conditions – had a clear criminal record. The applicant's criminal record was tainted due to his prior criminal conviction for refusing military service for reasons of conscience. In *Thlimmenos v. Greece*, the ECtHR said that:

> as a matter of principle, States have a legitimate interest to exclude some offenders from the profession of chartered accountant. However, the Court also considers that, unlike other convictions for serious criminal offences, a conviction for refusing on religious or philosophical grounds to wear the military uniform cannot imply any dishonesty or moral

---

181. See, for example, CZE-1995-3-010 a) Czech Republic / b) Constitutional Court / c) Fourth Chamber / d) 18-09-1995 / e) IV. US 81/95 / f) Conscientious Objectors and the Duty to Perform National Service / g) 4 *Sbírka zákonů* (Official Gazette), 50 / h) Codices (Czech), as reaffirmed in CZE-1997-3-009 a) Czech Republic / b) Constitutional Court / c) First Chamber / d) 14-10-1997 / e) I. US 322/96 / f) Repeated Conviction for the Criminal Offence of the Evasion of Military Service / g) / h) Codices (Czech). Note that in these cases the Czech Constitutional Court enforced the principle of *ne bis in idem* over the objection of the Czech Supreme Court.
182. *Ülke v. Turkey*, Application No. 39437/98, judgment of 24 January 2006.

turpitude likely to undermine the offender's ability to exercise this profession. Excluding the applicant on the ground that he was an unfit person was not, therefore, justified. The Court takes note of the Government's argument that persons who refuse to serve their country must be appropriately punished. However, it also notes that the applicant did serve a prison sentence for his refusal to wear the military uniform. In these circumstances, the Court considers that imposing a further sanction on the applicant was disproportionate.[183]

This decision was reached as a result of the joint application of Article 9 on freedom of religion and Article 14 on the prohibition of discrimination.

As constitutional jurisprudence demonstrates, refusal of armed service in the military may interfere with an individual's prospect for obtaining a hunting or weapons licence. In this respect it is useful to consider the German Constitutional Court's decision in the case where the applicant, a conscientious objector and pacifist, refused to take a shooting test in order to obtain a hunting licence for practising falconry. In this case, the German court agreed with exempting the applicant from the shooting test, submitting that taking such a test would violate the applicant's freedom of action under the Basic Law (Article 2(1)).[184] This judicial stance is best seen in the light of the decision of the Slovak Constitutional Court in a case where the justices invalidated a gun licensing law which prevented persons who undertook alternative service on grounds of conscientious objection from later holding a gun licence. In this case, the Slovak Constitutional Court applied the Constitution's Article 14.2 which provides that "No person shall be prevented from exercising his or her fundamental rights and freedoms." According to the Slovak Court, the lawful exercise of a constitutional right can result

---

183. *Thlimmenos v. Greece*, Application No. 34369/97, judgment of 6 April 2000, paragraph 47. The applicant was a Jehovah's Witness.
184. BVerfGE 55, 159. Summarised in English in Kommers, *Constitutional Jurisprudence*, p. 315.

in the deprivation from enjoying another right in the future.[185] Although the two cases differ largely on their face, it is a common element in both cases that – instead of relying on various aspects of free exercise – conscientious objectors' constitutional claims were fortified by being placed under the umbrella of more encompassing liberty claims.

Although conscientious objection is an important aspect of the free exercise of religion, it is not an internationally recognised human right, nor is it afforded protection as such under the ECHR. One of the reasons for the resistance to allow an exemption for conscientious objectors from military service under Article 9 is structural: while Article 9 does protect freedom of religion, conscientious objectors are mentioned in the context of slavery and forced labour, under Article 3(b), and the relationship of these provisions is still unresolved.[186] So far the ECtHR decided cases concerning the rights of conscientious objectors on grounds other than freedom of religion.[187] Despite such ambiguities, commentators indicate a general trend in international human rights law towards accepting a right to conscientious objection.[188]

General Comment No. 22 acknowledged already in 1993 that although the ICCPR does not expressly mention a right to conscientious objection, "such a right can be derived from article 18, inasmuch as the obligation to use lethal force may seriously conflict with the freedom of conscience and the right to manifest one's religion or belief."[189] Over the years, the Parliamentary Assembly of the Council of Europe have adopted several non-binding instruments encouraging the member states to adopt legislation.[190] Current concerns

---

185. SVK-1998-2-005 a) Slovakia / b) Constitutional Court / c) Plenary / d) 28-05-1998 / e) PL. US 18/97 / f) Petition from members of Parliament / g) *Zbierka zákonov Slovenskej republiky* (Official Gazette), 209/1998, in brief; *Zbierka nálezov a uznesen Ústavného súdu Slovenskej republiky* (Official Digest), in complete version / h) Codices (Slovak).
186. Evans, C., *Freedom of Religion*, pp. 170-173.
187. See Ovey and White, *The European Convention on Human Rights*, p. 314.
188. For a recent decision concerning a conscientious objector's complaint about repeated criminal convictions heard under the prohibition of inhuman treatment (Article 3), see *Ülke v. Turkey*.
189. Taylor, *Freedom of Religion*, p. 153.
190. *General Comment No. 22*, paragraph 11.

are enshrined well in Article 5 of Recommendation 1518 (2001), when the Parliamentary Assembly recommends legislation on the following:

1. the right to be registered as a conscientious objector at any time: before, during or after conscription, or performance of military service;
2. the right for permanent members of the armed forces to apply for the granting of conscientious objector status;
3. the right for all conscripts to receive information on conscientious objector status and the means of obtaining it;
4. genuine alternative service of a clearly civilian nature, which should be neither deterrent nor punitive in character.

The European Union's enlargement negotiations contribute positively to the acknowledgement of the claims of conscientious objectors. Most recently the European Parliament called on Turkey in a resolution to prepare a new legal framework recognising conscientious objection and welcomed Turkish efforts to introduce alternative military service.[191]

Even such a short overview of conscientious objection cannot be complete without recalling Harlan Friske Stone's words, reminding us that "liberty of conscience has a moral and social value which makes it worthy of preservation at the hands of the state. So deep in its significance and vital, indeed, is it to the integrity of man's moral and spiritual nature that nothing short of the self-preservation of the state should warrant its violation; and it may well be questioned whether the state which preserves its life by a settled policy of violation of the conscience of the individual will not in fact ultimately lose it by the process."[192]

---

191. Resolution 337 (1967) of the Parliamentary Assembly on the right of conscientious objection, adopted on 26 January 1967, Recommendation 1518 (2001) of the Parliamentary Assembly on the exercise of the right of conscientious objection to military service in Council of Europe member states, adopted on 23 May 2001, European Parliament Resolution of 7 February 1983 on conscientious objection, and also Committee of Ministers Recommendation No. R (87) 8 (9 EHRR (1987) 529), along with Explanatory Report to Recommendation No. R (87) 8.
192. Stone, H. F., "The Conscientious Objector," 21, *Columbia University, Quarterly*, 253, 1919, p. 269.

Chapter 3
Rights of religious communities and associations

Religious freedom has several important manifestations which commit believers to exercise their rights in community with others, very often within the framework of a religious organisation or association. Freedom of religion as an individual right is discussed typically as being a liberty interest or negative right, where the primary obligation of the state is to leave individuals undisturbed in the exercise of various aspects of religious freedom. When collective aspects of religious freedom are in the focus of attention, European scholars and lawyers instinctively turn to discuss the positive aspect of the right, namely, the obligation of the state to entrench or promote the enjoyment of religious freedom. Such accounts tend to put state–church relations in the centre of attention.

The US Constitution categorically prohibits the governmental establishment of religions, resulting in a tight separation of state and church not known in Europe.[193] Even in those European democracies which function without a state or majority church, or an official (or prevailing) religion, the constitutionally mandated separation of church and state permits differing forms of co-operation and co-existence between the state and religious organisations. This chapter explores how governmental interaction with religious

---

193. Note that such an active participation of the state in actively supporting religious exercise is not compatible with separation of church and state in the sense familiar to the US First Amendment jurisprudence. Due to the fundamental difference in underlying principles, US constitutional jurisprudence on separation of church and state is of limited utility for comparative analysis in the present chapter.

associations affects the exercise of religious freedoms through the lens of decisions of national courts performing constitutional review. It is important to note at the outset that religious freedoms are exercised by many believers in the framework of some organisation (association), and as the Krishnaswami study also notes, organisation is not always a matter of choice for believers.[194] While church membership might be seen as an essential or integral part of religious freedom, it is crucial to see the limitations on the exercise of religious freedom which may stem from governmental regulation of religious associations. As Cole Durham duly warns, the two variables along with the ambivalent relationship of religious freedom and church–state relations which may be assessed are the "degree to which state action burdens religious belief and conduct" and the "degree of identification between governmental and religious institutions."[195]

A proper comparative analysis of such a topic would on its own fill volumes, if not for any other reason than due to the differing constitutional regulations and historical experiences of European countries which deeply inform any regulation of church–state affairs. The current analysis is restricted to a few key problems which occupy constitutional courts and human rights protectors. While admitting at the outset that another selection of issues and problems would have been equally appropriate, following a short note on terminology, the first major section of this chapter offers an introduction to the most prevalent constitutional difficulties of governmental recognition or registration of religious associations. Then the chapter treats the complex relationship of religious freedom and public education in detail, while the last section is devoted to issues of accommodation in military and prison environments.

---

194. Krishnaswami, A., *Study of Discrimination in the Matter of Religious Rights and Practices*, U.N. Doc. E/CN.4/Sub.2/200/Rev.1, UN Sales No. 60. XIV.2, available at: http://www.religlaw.org/interdocs/docs/akstudy1960.htm.
195. Durham, W. C., Jr., "Perspectives of Religious Liberty, A Comparative Framework", pp. 1-42, in van der Vyver, J. D. and Witte, J., Jr., *Religious Human Rights in Global Perspective, Legal Perspectives*, Martinus Nijhoff, 1996, p. 15.

3.1. The basis of church–state relations: Registering religious associations

As Cole Durham reminds us, "a country's law and practice regarding religious entities constitutes a crucial test of its performance in facilitating freedom of religion or belief. ... The law governing the creation, recognition and registration of appropriate legal entities is vital for the life of most religious communities."[196] While religious freedom can be exercised in community with others without seeking the formal approval of the state, in modern democracies most religious communities aspire to obtain legal recognition, thus receiving legal personality and also allowing access to a wide range of benefits and services provided by the state.[197]

This section explores the intricacies and difficulties of seeking legal recognition for religious association, and constitutional limitations thereon as confirmed by European judicial review fora. Before entering a discussion of some of the most critical constitutional problems surrounding the official (formal) recognition or registration of religious communities, it is appropriate to acknowledge that most European legal systems distinguish between several types of religious organisations, often resulting in complicated, multi-tiered systems of legal recognition. Typically, religious associations are not able to choose one form or the other, but apply for the one which they are most likely to fit in the light of existing legal criteria. The intensity and appropriateness of justification for such differences in treatment vary in national constitutional approaches – sometimes thanks to extra-constitutional factors. The status quo in most national legal systems is not without problems as freedom of religion, freedom of association, the prohibition of discrimination, and the principle of state neutrality prevent governments from discriminating between denominations or religious organisations on the basis of the form of their incorporation.

---

196. Durham, W. C., Jr., "Facilitating Freedom of Religion or Belief through Religious Association Laws", pp. 321-405, in Lindholm, T., Durham, W. C., Jr., Tahzib-Lie, B. G., eds., *Facilitating Freedom of Religion or Belief: A Deskbook*, Martinus Nijhoff, 2004, p. 321.

197. Although there are a few religious communities which object to state recognition or registration as a matter of principle, the overwhelming majority of communities of believers would seek state approval in European democracies.

Freedom of religion

Case law

- ITA-1993-2-008 a) Italy / b) Constitutional Court / c) / d) 19-04-1993 / e) 195/1993 / f) / g) *Gazzetta Ufficiale, Prima Serie Speciale* (Official Gazette), 19, 05.05.1993 / h) Codices (Italian).

The intervention of public authorities in religious activities designed to facilitate the exercise of the right to worship – which is an expression of the fundamental and inviolable right to religious freedom explicitly guaranteed by Article 19 of the Constitution – must respect the supreme principle of the secular nature of the state, which is one of the characteristics of the form of state established by the Constitution.

All religious denominations are equally free before the law, including denominations which display no desire to establish an agreement with the state (Article 8.3 of the Constitution) or which have not succeeded in doing so, as well as denominations which take the form of simple communities of believers which are not regulated by special statutes.

Where the state intervenes in town planning matters to put up buildings or provide facilities intended for worship by allocating funds from urban taxes, the exclusion of a religious denomination from these advantages because it fails to meet the conditions laid down in Articles 8.2 and 8.3 of the Constitution, violates the first paragraph of the article in question. It is nonetheless clear that religious denominations do not automatically qualify for these advantages. Qualification can result simply from common regard, from public recognition or from the fact that a denomination qualifies by virtue of its status.

- *Moscow branch of the Salvation Army v. Russia*[198] Application No. 72881/01, Judgment of 5 October 2006

---

198. The struggle for the re-registration of the Moscow branch of the Salvation Army attracted the attention of the Council of Europe on several occasions in the past. Especially the Report of the Committee on the Honouring of Obligations and Commitments by Member States of the Council of Europe (Monitoring Committee, doc. 9396, 26 March 2002), paragraphs 95-104. Also, Parliamentary Assembly Resolution 1277 (2002) on the honouring of obligations and commitments by the Russian Federation, adopted on 23 April 2002 and Parliamentary Assembly Resolution 1278 (2002) on Russia's law on religion, adopted on 23 April 2002.

(The Salvation Army operated in Russia between 1913 and 1923, when it was dissolved for ant-Soviet activity. In 1992, it resumed its operations and successfully sought registration as a religious association and obtained legal personality. When the 1997 federal law on the freedom of conscience and religious associations, Law No. 125-FZ (the "Religions Act") came into force, the Moscow branch of the Salvation Army was refused re-registration. Domestic courts refused to re-register the Moscow branch of the Salvation Army.)

...

58. While religious freedom is primarily a matter of individual conscience, it also implies, *inter alia*, freedom to "manifest [one's] religion" alone and in private or in community with others, in public and within the circle of those whose faith one shares. Since religious communities traditionally exist in the form of organised structures, Article 9 must be interpreted in the light of Article 11 of the Convention, which safeguards associative life against unjustified State interference. Seen in that perspective, the right of believers to freedom of religion, which includes the right to manifest one's religion in community with others, encompasses the expectation that believers will be allowed to associate freely, without arbitrary State intervention. Indeed, the autonomous existence of religious communities is indispensable for pluralism in a democratic society and is thus an issue at the very heart of the protection which Article 9 affords. The state's duty of neutrality and impartiality, as defined in the Court's case law, is incompatible with any power on the state's part to assess the legitimacy of religious beliefs.

...

61. While in the context of Article 11 the Court has often referred to the essential role played by political parties in ensuring pluralism and democracy, associations formed for other purposes, including those proclaiming or teaching religion, are also important to the proper functioning of democracy. For pluralism is also built on the genuine recognition of, and respect for, diversity and the dynamics of cultural traditions, ethnic and cultural identities, religious beliefs, artistic, literary and socio-economic ideas and concepts. The harmonious interaction of persons and groups with varied identities is

essential for achieving social cohesion. It is only natural that, where a civil society functions in a healthy manner, the participation of citizens in the democratic process is to a large extent achieved through belonging to associations in which they may integrate with each other and pursue common objectives collectively.

62. The state's power to protect its institutions and citizens from associations that might jeopardise them must be used sparingly, as exceptions to the rule of freedom of association are to be construed strictly and only convincing and compelling reasons can justify restrictions on that freedom …

…

92. … It is undisputable that for the members of the applicant branch, using ranks similar to those used in the military and wearing uniforms were particular ways of organising the internal life of their religious community and manifesting the Salvation Army's religious beliefs.[199] It could not seriously be maintained that the applicant branch advocated a violent change of constitutional foundations or thereby undermined the integrity or security of the State …

…

96. … by the time the re-registration requirement was introduced, the applicant branch had lawfully existed and operated in Russia as an independent religious community for more than seven years. It has not been submitted that the community as a whole or its individual members had been

---

199. Author's note: See paragraph 18 of the decision: "On 12 July 2000 the Ministry of Education of the Russian Federation sent to education departments in Russian regions the instruction 'On Activities of Non-traditional Religious Associations in the Territory of the Russian Federation', which stated, in particular, as follows: 'in the Central part of Russia the international religious organisation the Salvation Army is expanding its activities. Its followers attempt to influence the youth and the military. The Salvation Army formally represents the Evangelical Protestant branch of Christianity, however, in essence, it is a quasi-military religious organisation that has a rigid hierarchy of management. The Salvation Army is managed and funded from abroad.'" The applicant branch submitted that this extract was copied verbatim from an information sheet prepared by the Federal Security Service of the Russian Federation and forwarded to the Ministry of Education on 29 May 2000.

in breach of any domestic law or regulation governing their associative life and religious activities. In these circumstances, the Court considers that the reasons for refusing re-registration should have been particularly weighty and compelling. In the present case no such reasons have been put forward by the domestic authorities.

Commentary

Fundamental premises of religious association law

A critical, problem-oriented discussion on the relationship of the state and religious associations shall be explained through a few basic premises. While all member states of the Council of Europe proclaim adherence to religious freedom, a few retain a state church. Having a state church, however, does not absolve national governments from respecting and protecting religious freedom.[200] As General Comment No. 22 points out:

> The fact that a religion is recognised as a state religion or that it is established as official or traditional or that its followers comprise the majority of the population, shall not result in any impairment of the enjoyment of any of the rights under the Covenant ... nor in any discrimination against adherents to other religions or non-believers. In particular, certain measures discriminating against the latter, such as measures restricting eligibility for government service to members of the predominant religion or giving economic privileges to them or imposing special restrictions on the practice of other faiths, are not in accordance with the prohibition of discrimination based on religion or belief and the guarantee of equal protection.[201]

Nonetheless, the European Court of Human Rights (ECtHR) was noticed to be rather reluctant in cases where applicants challenge

---

200. See Evans, C., *Freedom of Religion under the European Convention on Human Rights*, Oxford, 2001, pp. 80 et seq. An important exposition on the obligations of the state to protect freedom of religion in a state church system is found in the European Commission's decision in *Darby v. Sweden*, Application No. 11581/85, Rep. 1989.
201. *General Comment No. 22: The right to freedom of thought, conscience and religion*, Article 18, 30/07/93. CCPR/C/21/Rev.1/Add. (1993), paragraph 9.

the privileged position of established, traditional or historic churches in the member states.[202]

There is no definitive answer on whether the right to form a religious association may be derived from freedom of religion alone, or from freedom and freedom of association.[203] Differences in opinion may give rise to differing understandings on what amounts to a permissible justification concerning permissible limitations imposed upon religious associations. Yet, as seen in European constitutional case law and also in Strasbourg jurisprudence, the right to the collective exercise of religious freedom (collective worship) does not automatically entail a right to form an officially recognised or registered religious organisation, nor does it impose a duty on states to establish a special legal framework for such a purpose.[204] Governments retain broad discretion in establishing recognition mechanisms for religious associations. Official recognition usually results in access to legal entity status,[205] but it is important to remember that it does not automatically entail a right to state funding in most legal systems. Despite this broad leeway, it is worth noting that the more complex a registration system is (with multiple forms of recognised status established depending on differing access conditions), the higher the likelihood of unequal treatment of religious communities, and – ultimately – undue limitations on religious freedom.[206]

---

202. Gunn, T. J., "Adjudicating Rights of Conscience under the European Convention on Human Rights", pp. 305-330, in van der Vyver, J. and Witte, J., Jr., eds, *Religious Human Rights in Global Perspective, Legal Perspectives*, Martinus Nijhoff, 1996, p. 329. Analysing ECtHR jurisprudence, Gunn also points out an impermissible bias against non-mainstream and non-Christian religions, pp. 327-8.
203. See, for example, *Hasan and Chaush v. Bulgaria*, Application No. 30985/96, Judgment of 26 October 2000, paragraph 62 and *Metropolitan Church of Bessarabia v. Moldova*, Application No. 45701/99, Judgment of 13 December 2001, paragraph 118. For an analysis of these cases see Durham, *Facilitating Freedom of Religion*, pp. 366-372.
204. *X. v. Austria*, Application No. 8652/1979, 26 DR 89 (1981).
205. Durham, *Facilitating Freedom of Religion*, p. 392.
206. See, for example, Opinion No. 391/2006 on the draft law on the insertion of amendments on freedom of conscience and religious organisations in Ukraine, Adopted by the Venice Commission at its 68th Plenary Session (Venice, 13-14 October 2006), CDL-AD(2006)030, paragraph 39.

Nonetheless, once a state introduces a registration system or otherwise recognises beliefs for the purposes applying legal rules, it shall operate in a non-discriminatory fashion. Furthermore, the principle of non-discrimination should also be observed beyond the administration of the registration process. As the German Constitutional Court put it: "Beneficiaries of the fundamental right to religious freedom may – as a consequence of the religious and ideological neutrality of the state and the principle of equality of churches and confessions – be members not only of officially recognised churches but also of other religious communities" (Decision GER-1971-R-002 Germany / b) Federal Constitutional Court / c) First Panel / d) 19-10-1971 / e) 1 BvR 387/65 / f) / g) *Entscheidungen des Bundesverfassungsgerichts* (Official Digest), 32, 98, 266 / h)). In order to foreclose opportunities for discrimination between registered and non-registered churches the Macedonian Constitutional Court invalidated statutory provisions which required non-registered religious organisations to seek prior authorisation from the Ministry of Interior for holding religious ceremonies in places accessible to the public (Decision MKD-1999-3-010 a) "The former Yugoslav Republic of Macedonia" / b) Constitutional Court / c) / d) 10-11-1999 / e) U.br.114/99 / f) / g) *Sluzben vesnik na Republika Makedonija* (Official Gazette), 76/99 / h) Codices (Macedonian)). Distinctions between registered and non-registered religious associations are permissible to the extent that they live up to constitutional standards justifying limitations on religious freedom and unequal treatment.

Based upon the aforementioned, it is appropriate to conclude that a comprehensive analysis of the status of religious freedom under national church registration systems should not simply enquire into how difficult it is to get registration as a church (or any particular genre of religious organisation acknowledged in a state), but rather how difficult it is to obtain such legal status which is essential for an unhindered exercise of the religious freedom.[207]

Registration of religious associations is a double-edged sword. It may serve the purpose of facilitating religious freedom, yet it

---

207. On the scope of religious freedom see, for example, Article 6 of the Declaration on the Elimination of Intolerance and Discrimination Based on Religion or Belief, proclaimed by General Assembly Resolution 36/55 of 25 November 1981, on quote in Chapter 2.

may also become a means of governmental control over religious exercise.[208] In European democracies, official recognition or registration of religious organisations is claimed to be used to promote free religious exercise. Registration typically stands as a precondition of receiving access to government-provided opportunities and assistance in the hope to promote the exercise of freedom of religion. Religious organisations are motivated to seek recognition in order to be able to become recipients of such state-provided benefits.

Even in countries where a state church is not established, and where the government claims to observe the requirements of equal treatment and state neutrality in matters of faith, the intensity of legal recognition (and its consequences) tends to favour those churches which are understood (at least by an elite or a majority) to have contributed to the formation of the history, identity, culture or other underlying values of the polity. Such a legal framework is supportive of certain creeds over others, and runs the risk of becoming an instrument of government-sponsored discrimination. Thus, as even such a quick intervention suggests, the line between control and facilitation may be easily blurred in practice.

An overview of problems with conditions applicable to recognising religious organisations

The *OSCE-Venice Commission guidelines for review of legislation pertaining to religion or belief* identify the following major problems areas in European religious association law:[209]

- Registration of religious organisations should not be mandatory, although it is appropriate to require registration for the purposes of obtaining legal personality and similar benefits;
- Individuals and groups should be free to practise their religion without registration if they so desire;

---

208. This distinction is adopted from Durham, *Facilitating Freedom of Religion*, pp. 332 et seq.
209. *OSCE-Venice Commission guidelines for review of legislation pertaining to religion or belief*, p. 17, available at: http://www.osce.org/publications/odihr/2004/09/12361_142_en.pdf.

- High minimum membership requirements should not be allowed with respect to obtaining legal personality;

- It is not appropriate to require lengthy existence in the state before registration is permitted;

...

- Provisions that grant excessive governmental discretion in giving approvals should not be allowed; ...

- Intervention in internal religious affairs by engaging in substantive review of ecclesiastical structures, imposing bureaucratic review or restraints with respect to religious appointments, and the like, should not be allowed;

- Provisions that operate retroactively or that fail to protect vested interests (for example, by requiring re-registration of religious entities under new criteria) should be questioned.

...

These principles resonate the words of the ECtHR in *Hasan and Chaush v. Bulgaria*, when reminding us that "but for very exceptional cases, the right to freedom of religion as guaranteed under the Convention excludes any discretion on the part of the State to determine whether religious beliefs or the means used to express such beliefs are legitimate."[210]

Constitutions usually do not prescribe conditions for recognising religious associations. Compared to others, the German Basic Law's Weimar clauses awarding public law corporation status to religious associations are elaborate, when they provide that religious societies shall be granted such a status "if their constitution and the number of their members give assurance of their permanency. If two or more religious societies established under public law unite into a single organization, it too shall be a corporation under public law" (Article 137.5). When applied in practice, this results in the rather flexible criteria of "a minimum of organizational form, a consensus on the meaning of human existence, and bearing witness

---

210. *Hasan and Chaush v. Bulgaria*, p. 78. Note that the same sentence appeared before in *Manoussakis v. Greece*, Application No. 18748/91, judgment of 26 September 1996, paragraph 47, without the introductory qualification.

to that consensus."[211] Registration of religious associations is by no means required in Germany and there is no separate church register in Germany.[212] Religious associations which do not qualify for public law corporation status may still seek recognition under the German Civil Code as registered associations.[213]

While a solution for awarding legal recognition for religious associations exists in most European legal systems, not all countries have a special statute for general-purpose church registration. In such legal systems religious organisations are recognised for a particular purpose such as to gain charitable status (e.g. United Kingdom[214]), tax exemptions (e.g. France, Germany), permits to operate a house of worship (e.g. Greece[215]) or the power to officiate marriages (e.g. Denmark[216]). The following paragraphs will highlight some of those problems which persist in legal solutions throughout Europe. While problems are often explained in the light of differing historical backgrounds and national experiences, there are a few recurring

---

211. In Schoen, B., "New Religions in Germany, The Publicity of the Public Square", pp. 85-98, in: Lucas, P. C. and Robbins, T., eds, *New Religious Movements in the 21st Century, Legal, Political and Social Challenges in Global Perspective*, Routledge, 2004, p. 87.

212. On the consequences of public law corporation status, see Robbers, G., "Religious Freedom in Germany", 2001, *Brigham Young University Law Review*, 643, 2001, p. 651.

213. Note that in the *Ritual Slaughter case*, discussed in Section 2.2, the German Federal Constitutional Court found that for the purposes of the Animal Protection Act (Article 4a.1) two or more persons sharing a faith can be considered a religious community. This solution was not only instrumental to the success of the case, but is also believed to be capable of accommodating Muslim communities. See Zacharias, D. "Access of Muslim Organisations to Religious Instruction in Public Schools: A Comment on the Decision of the Federal Administrative Court of 23 February 2005", 6(10), *German Law Journal*, 1320, 2005, p. 1326.

214. See Cumper, P., "Religious Liberty in the United Kingdom", 205-242, in van der Vyver, J. and Witte, J., Jr., eds, *Religious Human Rights in Global Perspective: Legal Perspectives*, Martinus Nijhoff, 1996, p. 219.

215. On this see *Manoussakis and Others v. Greece*. For the application of the Places of Worship Registration Act, 1885, in the United Kingdom see Cumper, "Religious Liberty in the United Kingdom", p. 221.

216. On this see Dübeck, I., "State and Church in Denmark", pp. 37-56, in Robbers, G., ed., *State and Church in the European Union*, Nomos, 1996, p. 42. For a list of recognised religions in English see *Denmark, International Religious Freedom Report 2006*, at: http://www.state.gov/g/drl/rls/irf/2006/71377.htm.

traits in these cases which are worth pointing out before turning to a detailed analysis of jurisprudence.[217]

To begin with, the protection of religious freedom and freedom of association, and also the requirement of equal treatment should guide legislators to adopt a solution under which the recognition of registration of religious associations is not more burdensome than the registration of any other (civic) association. Departures from this basic premise result in otherwise easily avoidable violations of constitutional rights.

Furthermore, one must be mindful of the fact that even the most formal, objective or neutral assessment criteria of registration or recognition are applied with reference to value judgments. In *Church of the New Faith v. Commissioner of Pay-Roll Tax (Victoria)*, Murphy J. of the Australian High Court said that "administrators and judges must resist the temptation to hold that groups or institutions are not religious because claimed religious beliefs or practices seem absurd, fraudulent, evil or novel; or because the group or institution is new, the number of adherents small, the leaders hypocrites, or because they seek to obtain the financial and other privileges which come with religious status."[218] To this, Mason ACJ added that "charlatanism is a necessary price of religious freedom."[219]

Registration as a precondition of collective religious exercise

Legal rules which make the legal exercise of religious freedom subject to prior registration impose a rather heavy burden on constitutional rights. Examples are rare in Europe, but not inexistent.[220]

---

217. Prohibitions on religious political parties will not be discussed due to spatial limitations.
218. *Church of the New Faith v. Commissioner of Pay-Roll Tax (Victoria)* (1983) 154 CLR 120, 150. The issue in the case was whether the Church of Scientology was entitled to a tax exemption.
219. *Church of the New Faith v. Commissioner of Pay-Roll Tax (Victoria)* (1983), 141.
220. Note that the Serbian draft law on religious associations for making the exercise of religious freedom dependent on the registration of religious associations was criticised by the Venice Commission for leaving no room for the *forum internum*. See Opinion No. 334/2005, comments on the draft law on religious organisations in Serbia by Mr Peter Jambrek (Member, Slovenia), 3 March 2005, CDL(2005)026, at http://www.venice.coe.int/docs/2005/CDL(2005)026-e.asp.

In Belarus, all religious organisations are subject to registration in order to operate in a legal fashion.[221] Also, under Moldovan law religious denominations may only proceed with their operations following registration.[222] When the Metropolitan Church of Bessarabia challenged the Moldovan government's failure to register it, the ECtHR said that "the right of believers to freedom of religion, which includes the right to manifest one's religion in community with others, encompasses the expectation that believers will be allowed to associate freely, without arbitrary State intervention."[223] The ECtHR found that the failure of the Moldovan authorities to register the Metropolitan Church of Bessarabia under the act as in force violated Article 9. In this case, the ECtHR noted that "the Court cannot regard [tolerance towards religious organisations] as a substitute for recognition, since recognition alone is capable of conferring rights on those concerned."[224] In 2001, the Spanish Constitutional Court also acknowledged that obtaining registration is an important aspect of constitutionally protected religious freedom.[225]

The deferential stance of the ECtHR is unfortunate as similar problems surface in other jurisdictions. In Bulgaria – where religious organisations were not required to register before – the 2002 Religious Denominations Act[226] introduced a fine on the exercise of unrecognised religions and allows for the dissolution of unrecognised religious groups (Article 38). The act recognises the Bulgarian

---

221. Article 16.1, on Introduction of Changes and Amendments to the Law of the Republic of Belarus on Freedom of Conscience and Religious Organisations, Law of the Republic of Belarus, 137-3 of 5 November 2002/12 November 2002. Available in English at http://religlaw.org/template.php?id=1367.
222. Article 14.5, Law of the Republic of Moldova on Denominations, No. 979-XII, as available in English at: http://religlaw.org/template.php?id=1758.
223. *Metropolitan Church of Bessarabia v. Moldova*, paragraph 118.
224. *Metropolitan Church of Bessarabia v. Moldova*, paragraph 129. Nonetheless, the ECtHR did not go so far in the case as to find that the entire registration model violated religious freedom.
225. STC, 15 February 2001 (S.T.C., No. 46/2001), as explained in Motilla, A., "Religious Pluralism in Spain: Striking the Balance between Religious Freedom and Constitutional Rights", 2004, *Brigham Young University Law Review*, 575, 2004, p. 589. The case involved the registration of the Unification Church.
226. Religious Denominations Act, Issue No. 120, State Gazette. As available in English at: http://religlaw.org/template.php?id=1368.

Eastern-Orthodox Church as a traditional denomination, adding that "It has played a historic role in Bulgaria's statehood and has current meaning in its political life" (Article 10.1). While the act also mentions the opportunity for registering other religious organisations (Article 14 et seq.), it does not disclose criteria of evaluation of any such application,[227] nor does it prescribe the consequences of a rejected registration request.[228] In 2003, the Bulgarian Constitutional Court upheld the law,[229] which was heavily criticised inside and outside Bulgaria. As a major action against unregistered religions, in the summer of 2004, police invaded over 250 places belonging to the Alternative Orthodox Synod, an organisation which was not recognised under the 2002 law.[230] This campaign should be assessed in the light of the fact that the very purpose of the 2002 act was to remove the schism within the Orthodox Church.

---

227. Note that the Slovenian act on the legal status of religious associations does not include criteria of registration either. As reported in Sturm, L., "Church–state Relations and the Legal Status of Religious Communities in Slovenia", 2004, *Brigham Young University Law Review*, 607, 2004, p. 625.
228. For the history and basic overview of the Denominations Act, see Kanev, K.,"Law and Politics toward the Muslims in Bulgaria", pp. 316-344, in: Danchin, P. G. and Cole, E. A., eds, *Protecting the Human Rights of Religious Minorities in Eastern Europe*, Columbia, 2002, and Panov, L., "The New Law on Religious Denominations in Bulgaria", at http://www.efc.be/cgi-bin/articlepublisher.pl?filename=LP-SE-06-03-1.html.
229. Decision No. 12 of 15 July 2003 on constitutional case No. 3/2003. An English-language summary is available with the website of the Bulgarian Constitutional Court at: http://www.constcourt.bg/sum-en-2003.htm.
230. See Amnesty International's 2004 report on Bulgaria at: http://web.amnesty.org/report2005/bgr-summary-eng.

Proving social acceptance: membership criteria

Thus, although a statutory framework[231] prescribing the conditions of eligibility for religious association status is usually regarded as an important safeguard of religious freedom, on its own it might be insufficient to safeguard religious freedom. Statutory conditions of registration which are prohibitively difficult to meet (may they require a large number of founders, frequent re-registration or overly complicated assurances), legal requirements of registration which on their face seem to purposely prefer particular types of creeds to the detriment of others,[232] or – to the contrary – the complete lack of any disclosed registration criteria applied in a discretionary fashion and without judicial control, are all indicators of a state's inclinations to use a registration process as a means of excessive governmental control or discrimination.[233]

When national rules require a sizeable group to file for or request registration, it is often explained in facially neutral terms as a means to test the social acceptance of a religious group. With requiring 20 000 permanent residents to file a request, Slovak law sets an

---

231. The lack of statutory regulation of registration criteria does not necessarily mean that such conditions are missing. In Belgium, criteria of recognition were defined in the following terms by the Minister of Justice in the 2000-2001 legislative session upon a question concerning the recognition of Buddhism: "(a) relatively high number of members (several tens of thousands), (b) being structured, which means the presence of a representative body which is in the position to represent the denomination in its contacts with the government, (c) being present in the country for a fairly long period of time, which means several decennia, (d) representing some social interest, (e) abstention on any activity contrary to the social order." Torfs, R., "On the Permissible Scope of Legal Limitations on the Freedom of Religion or Belief in Belgium", 19, *Emory International Law Review*, 637, 2005, pp. 661-662.

232. Note that certain religious communities operate in small congregations which fall below such high thresholds. As was pointed out in the Krishnaswami study, "in a case where the law prescribes a minimum membership for forming a religious association, but the religion itself considers fewer members to be sufficient for this purpose, a small group may be handicapped in its desire to organize."

233. For example, new religious movements reportedly suffered a disadvantage in Spain when the government agency responsible for registering religious associations applied the relevant legal rules with exercising improper discretion, prompting the Constitutional Court to put an end to this practice. In Motilla, "Religious Pluralism in Spain", pp. 588-589.

unusually high limit for those religious communities which are not exempted *ex lege* from the registration requirement.[234]

In the 1998 Austrian law supplementing the 1874 act on religious organisations, a relatively high threshold is set for registration of previously unrecognised religions.[235] A newly introduced "confessional community" (which is a lesser degree religious association) takes 300 residents to establish (Section 3.3). In order to qualify as a religion in terms of the 1874 law, however, a confessional community must have a membership of 0.2% of the population, meaning about 16 000 members (Section 11). "Only four of the thirteen recognized religious (Catholic, Protestant, Islamic Community, and Eastern Orthodox) groups would meet this membership requirement. Of the unrecognized religious groups, only the Jehovah's Witnesses would meet this latter membership requirement."[236] Jehovah's Witnesses challenged the procedure brought by the 1998 Austrian law in a case which the ECtHR found admissible in 2005.[237] While several national legal systems impose lower thresholds for registering a religious association (e.g. Hungary and Poland require 100 founders), few are close to the ideal advocated recently by the Parliamentary Assembly and also the Venice Commission, setting

---

234. See Article 11 in Law on the Freedom of Religious Belief and on the Status of Churches and Religious Societies, Law No. 308/1991, as available in English at http://religlaw.org/template.php?id=1763 and Amendment to Act No. 308/1991 on the Freedom of Religious Expression and the Status of Churches and Religious Societies, Act No. 394/2000 Coll. Of 31 October 2000, as available in English at http://religlaw.org/template.php?id=1. The appendix to the law contains a list of 15 exempted religious associations, including Seventh Day Adventists and Jehovah's Witnesses.

235. Law on the Status of Religious Communities for confessional communities (*Rechtspersönlichkeit von religiösen Bekenntnisgemeinshaften*, 19/1998. The old statute is the Recognition Act (*Anerkennungsgesetz* (1874)).

236. *Austria, International Religious Freedom Report*, 2006, at: http://www.state.gov/g/drl/rls/irf/2006/71367.htm.
For an overview of the practical impact of the Austrian registration system, see Annex III to a report of Human Rights without Frontiers, by Fautré, W., "Fighting religious segregation and discrimination against minority religions and their members in the OSCE space", at: http://www.osce.org/documents/cio/2005/06/15270_en.pdf.

237. *Religionsgemeinschaft der zeugen Jehovas in Österreich, Franz Aigner, Kurt Binder, Karl Kopenzy and Johann Renoldner v. Austria*, Application No. 40825/98.

the same standard for the registration of religious associations as is applicable to other associations.[238]

Mandatory waiting periods

Mandatory waiting periods are also seen in national legal rules, often as preconditions for obtaining recognition at an advanced level. Although imposing a low membership requirement, Latvian law requires new religions to re-register annually for the first 10 years of operation in the country, so that national authorities can monitor the legality of their functioning (Article 8.4).[239] In addition to a critically high membership requirement under the 1998 Austrian law, the applicant confessional community must be organised for 20 years, out of which 10 must be spent in the form of a confessional community in the terms prescribed in the new law (Section 11).[240] Also, Portugal's 2001 religious freedom act requires for the registration of a church 30 years of presence in Portugal, or alternatively, 60 years of international presence.[241] Although the Church of Scientology has been recognised in Portugal since 1986, it does not benefit from the new act.[242]

---

238. See Opinion No. 391/2006 on the draft law on the insertion of amendments on freedom of conscience and religious organisations in Ukraine, adopted by the Venice Commission at its 68th Plenary Session (Venice, 13-14 October 2006), CDL-AD(2006)030, paragraph 38.
    To this effect see also MKD-1998-3-009 a) "The former Yugoslav Republic of Macedonia" / b) Constitutional Court / c) / d) 24-12-1998 / e) U.br.223/97 / f) / g) *Sluzben vesnik na Republika Makedonija* (Official Gazette, 64/98) / h).
239. Under Article 7.1, 10 citizens of legal age can apply for registering a congregation. The monitoring period is set in Article 8.4, Law on Religious Organisations, adopted by the Parliament on 7 September 1995 and subsequently amended at numerous times, as available in English at: http://religlaw.org/template.php?id=1755.
240. A similar solution was introduced in 2002 in the Czech Republic Law on Churches and Religious Societies, No. 3/2002, available in English at: http://religlaw.org/template.php?id=1752. The act was amended in 2005.
241. Article 37.2 of Law No. 16/2001 of 21 June, Law on religious freedom. As available in English at: http://religlaw.org/template.php?id=415.
242. Portugal, *International Religious Freedom Report 2006*, at: http://www.state.gov/g/drl/rls/irf/2006/71401.htm.

A waiting period to a similar effect was introduced in Russia by the 1997 federal law on religious freedom,[243] under which religious organisations which cannot prove that their existence in Russia dates back at least 15 years were required to seek annual re-registration until the expiry of this 15-year term (Article 27.3.3). This rule imposed a burden on a number of new religious movements which were first registered in Russia under the previous law of 1990 regulating the registration of religious associations.[244] The Russian Constitutional Court held in 1999[245] that the re-registration provisions of the 1997 federal law did not apply to religious organisations which were already registered (under the old law) at the time the new law entered into force. Constitutional justices did not invalidate the challenged provisions of the 1997 federal law, but appended the above requirements as a condition of constitution-conform interpretation of the law.[246] Although the Constitutional Court reaffirmed this interpretation of the 1997 federal law on re-registration, ordinary courts were not willing to adhere to this reading of the law, giving rise to the *Moscow Branch of the Salvation Army v. Russia* case, quoted above at length.[247]

Such waiting periods are justified by assertions that benefits flowing from registration shall only be awarded to religious communities which enjoy minimal social acceptance, or that only serious groups shall qualify for officially recognised status. As even such a short

---

243. Law on the Freedom of Conscience and Religious Associations, Law No. 125-FZ (subsequently amended). As available in English at: http://religlaw.org/template.php?id=1762.
244. Law of the Russian Soviet Federative Socialist Republic on Freedom of Worship of 25 October 1990. As available in English at: http://religlaw.org/template.php?id=74.
245. Constitutional Court Decision of the Russian Federation concerning the constitutionality of the third and fourth paragraphs of Paragraph 3 of Article 27 of Federal Law "On Freedom of Conscience and Religious Associations", Moscow, 23 November 1999. As available in English (unofficial translation) at: http://religlaw.org/template.php?id=561.
246. The decision of the Constitutional Court also confirmed the conscientious objector status of one of the applicants, who was a Jehovah's Witness.
247. A similar re-registration scenario was behind the events in a Bulgarian case involving Jehovah's Witnesses which was resolved with a friendly settlement. *Lotter and Lotter v. Bulgaria*, Application No. 39015/97, judgment of 19 May 2004 (Friendly settlement).

overview suggests, mandatory waiting periods tend to adversely affect new religious movements.[248] In essence, these rules use the newness of a faith to limit believers' religious freedom – hardly a permissible ground for limiting a fundamental right.[249]

Further limitations of religious freedom stemming from legal definitions in regulations on religious association

There are several other conditions in national legal systems which particular religious communities may find difficult to meet, due to their religious doctrines. The requirement that members of a religious association shall follow a theistic creed is problematic not only for the Church of Scientology,[250] but also for Buddhist communities.

In Germany – under the otherwise rather flexible recognition system – Jehovah's Witnesses faced difficulties when applying for a public law corporation status, when the Federal Administrative Court required the association to be "loyal to the state". This requirement appears problematic as Jehovah's Witnesses are expected to refrain from participating in national elections and also object to all forms of military service. The German Constitutional Court rejected the condition imposed by the Federal Administrative Court, holding that in order to obtain a public law corporation status, Jehovah's Witnesses were supposed to be loyal to the law.[251]

---

248. Mandatory waiting periods are rather efficient in keeping new religious movements at bay, if combined with limitations on proselytisation and immigration (visa) restrictions.
249. Durham, *Facilitating Freedom of Religion*, p. 391.
250. See, for example, Lord Denning in *R. v. Registrar General, Ex p Segerdal*, [1970] 2 QB 697, p. 707 saying that "Turning to the creed of the Church of Scientology, I must say that it seems to me to be more a philosophy of the existence of man or of life, rather than a religion. Religious worship means reverence or veneration of God or of a supreme being." The case involved a request for the registration under the Places of Worship Registration Act 1855.
251. Reported in Robbers, G., "The Permissible Scope of Legal Limitations on The Freedom of Religion or Belief in Germany", 17, *Emory International Law Review*, 841, 2005, pp. 880-881. See also Eberle, E., "Free Exercise of Religion in Germany and the United States", 78, *Tulane Law Review*, 1023, 2004, p. 1031. Also discussed in Dorsen, et al., *Comparative Constitutionalism*, West, 2003, p. 1001.

Statutes which establish such legal schemes on the recognition of religious associations often expect religious organisation to have a highly organised and hierarchical structure. In certain legal systems this requirement appears in the definition of recognised religious institutions,[252] while more frequently it is simply one among the conditions for recognition. This approach might not fit non-Christian religions. Indeed, general definition aside, legal criteria for recognising a religious association tend to expect a highly organised structure in a religious community. As a result, in most European countries Muslim communities face difficulties, as very often they cannot designate one representative organisation which should negotiate with the state.[253] Although the example of the Spanish agreement shows that finding a representative of Muslim communities might not be completely impossible,[254] several European states are trying to establish other forms of communication and co-operation between the state and at least some Muslim religious associations which are based on continuous dialogue instead of one formalised agreement.

Church autonomy: The role of religious perspectives in registration processes

In the light of the above examples, it is apparent that unlike in cases involving individual religious freedoms, in these cases concerning religious association courts are reluctant to accept the understanding of organisations on their self-perception of being of an independent religious nature. Concluding its decision quoted above, the Italian Constitutional Court said that "it is not sufficient for the applicant to describe itself as a religious denomination, and that this must be verified in terms of previous public recognition of

---

252. For such a definition see, for example, the Belarus law (Article 3) and the Estonian Law (Articles 2.2 and 23.1).
253. See, for example, *Germany, International Religious Freedom Report 2006*, at: http://www.state.gov/g/drl/rls/irf/2006/71382.htm. Also, Concluding observations of the Human Rights Committee: Belgium. 12/08/2004. CCPR/CO/81/BEL. (Concluding Observations/Comments) (12 August 2004) paragraph 26.
254. Martínez-Torrón, J., "Religious Freedom and Democratic Change in Spain", *2006 Brigham Young University Law Review*, 777, 2006, pp. 800 et seq.

the status of the applicant, or at least by the way in which it was viewed by the general public."[255]

The *OSCE-Venice Commission guidelines on the registration of religious associations* emphasise that requirements of state neutrality are observed by such conditions which allow for a formal (instead of a substantive) review of applicant organisations' founding charters.[256] In addition to considerations of neutrality, this requirement may also be understood as a safeguard of autonomy of religious organisations. Within the framework of the present analysis there is little room to reflect on the scope and limits of church autonomy, a subject which has vast literature as well as rich jurisprudence. Nonetheless, in an account of registration procedures, it is important to draw attention to several implications of the (alleged or assumed) respect for autonomy of religious associations[257] which might result in the impairment of the religious freedoms of others.

The Greek Constitution confirms the Eastern Orthodox Church as a prevailing religion,[258] and provides for the unhindered exercise of "known religions" (Article 13.2). Although there is no formal registration procedure, several legal rules contain this phrase. In an attempt to clarify the boundaries of the concept, the Council of State stated that "in order to qualify as a religion or creed, it is irrelevant whether the creed constitutes a heresy in the eyes of the prevailing Orthodox religion; similarly, it is irrelevant that the followers of the creed do not have religious authorities or that their ministers do not belong to a priesthood" (Decision GRE-1975-R-001 a) Greece / b) Council of State / c) Assembly / d) 03-07-

---

255. Fourth periodic reports of States parties due in 1995: Italy. 28/05/97. CCPR/C/103/Add.4, at: http://www.unhchr.ch/tbs/doc.nsf/(Symbol)/35687b6e2729b5b7802565800055b605?Opendocument, paragraph 166.
256. *OSCE-Venice Commission guidelines on the registration of religious associations*, p. 11.
257. Van der Vyver uses the phrase "sphere sovereignty" in a similar manner. See van der Vyver, J. D., "The Relationship of Freedom of Religion or Belief Norms to Other Human Rights", pp. 85-123, in Lindholm, T., Durham, W. C. and Tahzib-Lie, B. G., eds, *Facilitating Freedom of Religion or Belief: A Deskbook*, Martinus Nijhoff, 2004, p. 94.
258. The concept of "prevailing religion" is explained in detail in Papastathis, Ch., "State and Church in Greece", pp. 75-92, in Robbers, G., ed., *State and Church in the European Union*, Nomos, 1996, pp. 77-78.

1975 / e) 2105/75 / f) / g) / h)). Nonetheless, in a subsequent case, the Council of State found that the community of believers who identify themselves as the "Followers of the Old Calendar" did not constitute a different creed from that of the Orthodox Church, as the only difference between the two communities was their position about which calendar to follow (Julian or Gregorian) (Decision GRE-1991-R-001 a) Greece / b) Council of State / c) Assembly / d) 03-05-1991 / e) 1444/91 / f) / g) / h)). Curiously, this conclusion (which ultimately prevented the religious community to have its own place of worship) coincided with that of the Orthodox Church which is not willing to acknowledge the Followers of the Old Calendar as followers of a distinct creed.[259] In the light of more recent ECtHR jurisprudence, however, this judicial approach is problematic. In the *Metropolitan Church of Bessarabia v. Moldova* case, the ECtHR said (para 123) that "by taking the view that the applicant Church was not a new denomination and by making its recognition depend on the will of an ecclesiastical authority that had been recognised – the Metropolitan Church of Moldova – the State failed to discharge its duty of neutrality and impartiality."

Note that while the ECtHR does accept state church systems, it has grown increasingly impatient with national legal rules which select officially acceptable ministers in the face of clear opposition from affected communities of believers. In *Serif v. Greece*, Greek courts found that a mufti who was elected by a community of believers yet was not appointed by the state under a special law resting on an international treaty exercising freedom of religion, was guilty of usurping the office of a minister of a "known religion", an offence under the Greek Criminal Code (Article 175.2). In response the ECtHR said that:

> [it] does not consider that, in democratic societies, the State needs to take measures to ensure that religious communities remain or are brought under a unified leadership...
>
> Although ... it is possible that tension is created in situations where a religious or any other community becomes divided,

---

259. On the schism in the Greek Orthodox Church and its relevance for the protection of religious freedom see, for example, Mavrogordatos, G. T., "Orthodoxy and Nationalism in the Greek Case," pp. 117-136, in Madeley, J. T. S. and Enyedi, Zs., eds, *Church and State in Contemporary Europe, The Chimera of Neutrality*, Frank Cass, 2003, p. 125.

it considers that this is one of the unavoidable consequences of pluralism. The role of the authorities in such circumstances is not to remove the cause of tension by eliminating pluralism, but to ensure that the competing groups tolerate each other.[260]

A similar conclusion was reached in *Hasan and Chaush v. Bulgaria*, which arose out of a challenge against the Bulgarian government's selection of a chief mufti – a governmental measure to control religious communities, dating back to 1992. In this case, the ECtHR stressed, that "State action favouring one leader of a divided religious community or undertaken with the purpose of forcing the community to come together under a single leadership against its own wishes would ... constitute an interference with freedom of religion."[261] Indeed, governmental interference caused lasting schism not only in Orthodox but also in Muslim communities, and ultimately fuelled the adoption of the 2002 Denominations Act. This law does not only fall short of the premises outlined in ECtHR jurisprudence,[262] but was recorded to further tensions between religious factions.[263]

---

260. *Serif v. Greece*, Application No. 38178/97, judgment of 14 December 1999, paragraphs 52-53.
    In this case, the ECtHR seems to have attributed significance to the fact that the unofficial mufti did not perform such acts which would have had legal consequences under Greek law (e.g. officiate marriages).
261. *Hasan and Chaush v. Bulgaria*, paragraph 78. See Ovey, C. and White, R. C. A., eds, Jacobs and White, *The European Convention on Human Rights*, fourth edition, Oxford, 2006, pp. 301-302, noting that thereby the ECtHR confirmed that Article 9 protects not only the rights of individuals, but also of religious associations.
262. Kanev, K., "Law and Politics toward the Muslims in Bulgaria", pp. 316-344, in: Danchin, P. G. and Cole, E. A., eds, *Protecting the Human Rights of Religious Minorities in Eastern Europe*, Columbia UP, 2002, pp. 339-340.
263. See *Human Rights in Bulgaria in 2003*, Annual Report of the Bulgarian Helsinki Committee, of April 2004, available at: http://www.bghelsinki.org/annual/en/2003.htm#5.

3.2. Education and religious instruction

Recommendation 1720 (2005) on education and religion[264] of the Parliamentary Assembly of the Council of Europe is concluded with the observation that:

> 6. Education is essential for combating ignorance, stereotypes and misunderstanding of religions. Governments should also do more to guarantee freedom of conscience and of religious expression, to foster education on religions, to encourage dialogue with and between religions and to promote the cultural and social expression of religions.

An analysis of the relationship of education and religion is expected to shed light on a number of competing, and sometimes conflicting considerations. Public education is a governmental function and a zone of public life over which control shifted from the established church to a secularised state.[265] Nonetheless, despite claims about separation of church and state, secularity or state neutrality (as the case may be, depending on the jurisdiction) governments in Europe are seen more and more often to co-operate with religious associations in organising the education sector and determining curricula. Government action is understood to pertain to the positive aspect of religious freedom. To the extent governments co-operate with traditional, registered or recognised religious associations, government action is often also problematic from an equal protection perspective.[266] In addition, in the highly regulated education environment, complaints about improper interference with individual religious freedoms are numerous, and the resolution of such claims depends on one's delineation of the *forum internum* and manifestation of religious freedom.[267] In the contexts of education, judicial analysis on permissible limitations of free religious exercise may be

---

264. Text adopted by the Assembly on 4 October 2005.
265. Rémond, R., *Religion and Society in Modern Europe*, translated by Antonia Nevill, Oxford, 1999, p. 147. For a comparison of liberal and Christian perspectives on the function of education see Adhar, R. and Leigh, I., *Religious Freedom in the Liberal State*, Oxford, 2005, pp. 227-233.
266. Furthermore, in countries with a multi-level registration system, typically a higher (not entry)-level registration is required for access to institutions of public education.
267. Evans, C., *Freedom of Religion*, pp. 88 et seq.

too easily overcast by considerations of a state's missions and its relatively broad discretion in setting standards in education. The following section explores several constitutional problems in religious education in public schools and in private denominational schools, while the last segment is devoted to exploring prohibitions on Islamic headscarves in public educational institutions.

> *Case law*
>
> ■ GER-1975-R-001 a) Germany / b) Federal Constitutional Court / c) First Panel / d) 17-12-1975 / e) 1 BvR 63/68 / f) / g) *Entscheidungen des Bundesverfassungsgerichts* (Official Digest), 41, 29 / h).
>
> Article 7 of the Basic Law leaves the democratic *Land* legislator to determine the religious/ideological character of public schools, having due regard to the fundamental right guaranteed by Article 4 of the Basic Law.
>
> The fundamental right guaranteed by Articles 4.1 and 4.2 of the Basic Law includes the right of parents to provide their children with the religious or ideological education which they consider proper.
>
> The democratic *Land* legislator has the task of resolving the inevitable tension between "negative" and "positive" freedom of religion in schools by reconciling the various legal interests protected by the constitution.
>
> A form of school which does everything possible to remove religious and ideological constraints, provides opportunities for objective discussion of all religious and ideological beliefs – even with Christian values as the basic reference point – and respects the requirement of tolerance in so doing, does not involve parents and children who reject religious education in a constitutionally unacceptable conflict of belief and conscience.
>
> ■ *Leyla Sahin v. Turkey*
> Application No. 44774/98, judgment of 10 November 2005
>
> (The applicant, a university student, violated a Turkish legal ban imposed on wearing a headscarf on university premises. When the ban was challenged before the ECtHR as a

violation of religious freedom under Article 9, the Court said the following:)

...

78. As to whether there was interference, the Grand Chamber endorses the following findings of the Chamber (see paragraph 71 of the Chamber judgment):

"The applicant said that, by wearing the headscarf, she was obeying a religious precept and thereby manifesting her desire to comply strictly with the duties imposed by the Islamic faith. Accordingly, her decision to wear the headscarf may be regarded as motivated or inspired by a religion or belief and, without deciding whether such decisions are in every case taken to fulfil a religious duty, the Court proceeds on the assumption that the regulations in issue, which placed restrictions of place and manner on the right to wear the Islamic headscarf in universities, constituted an interference with the applicant's right to manifest her religion."

...

109. Where questions concerning the relationship between State and religions are at stake, on which opinion in a democratic society may reasonably differ widely, the role of the national decision-making body must be given special importance. This will notably be the case when it comes to regulating the wearing of religious symbols in educational institutions, especially in view of the diversity of the approaches taken by national authorities on the issue ... Rules in this sphere will consequently vary from one country to another according to national traditions and the requirements imposed by the need to protect the rights and freedoms of others and to maintain public order. Accordingly, the choice of the extent and form such regulations should take must inevitably be left up to a point to the State concerned, as it will depend on the domestic context concerned.

110. This margin of appreciation goes hand in hand with a European supervision embracing both the law and the decisions applying it. The Court's task is to determine whether the measures taken at national level were justified in principle and proportionate. In delimiting the extent of the margin of appreciation in the present case the Court must have regard

> to what is at stake, namely the need to protect the rights and freedoms of others, to preserve public order and to secure civil peace and true religious pluralism, which is vital to the survival of a democratic society.
>
> ...
>
> 116... . it is the principle of secularism, as elucidated by the (Turkish) Constitutional Court, which is the paramount consideration underlying the ban on the wearing of religious symbols in universities. In such a context, where the values of pluralism, respect for the rights of others and, in particular, equality before the law of men and women are being taught and applied in practice, it is understandable that the relevant authorities should wish to preserve the secular nature of the institution concerned and so consider it contrary to such values to allow religious attire, including, as in the present case, the Islamic headscarf, to be worn.
>
> ...

Commentary

Introduction: parental rights and state duties

Education-related rights are the rights of parents (or legal guardians), but not of children.[268] This is clear not only from the language of the Universal Declaration on Human Rights (Article 26.3) and Article 18(4) of the ICCPR (on quote in Chapter 1), but also from Article 2 of Protocol No.1 to the ECHR,[269] which provides that:

> No person shall be denied the right to education. In the exercise of any functions which it assumes in relation to education and to teaching, the State shall respect the right of parents to ensure such education and teaching in conformity with their own religions and philosophical convictions.

---

268. Evans, M. D., *Religious Liberty and International Law in Europe*, Cambridge, 1997, p. 346, noting that while the child is the beneficiary, she does not have an independent right.
269. On the drafting history see Evans, C., *Freedom of Religion*, pp. 45 et seq. Also Evans, M., *Religious Liberty*, pp. 273, 342.

As explained in the light of its drafting history, under the ECHR – although access to private education is an important form of providing access to religious education under the ECHR – parents are not entitled to funding for any particular kind of religious education.[270] Most importantly, however, parents are vested with a right to claim protection against governmental religious indoctrination in education.[271] As Malcolm Evans reminds us, in the light of Strasbourg jurisprudence, the prohibition on indoctrination is to be understood narrowly: parents may not object to religious education which provides information on religions in a general, objective or comparative manner.[272] This is especially important when one realises that numerous cases involve claims for exemption from a particular form of denominational instruction with reference to the parents' individual convictions.

Such as in other areas, in matters of religious education parental choices may be counterbalanced in the "best interest" of the child, an important principle enshrined in the Declaration of the Rights of the Child (principle 7).[273] This fine balance between parental rights and the child's best interest also underscores the 1981 Declaration in Article 5.2 providing that:

> Every child shall enjoy the right to have access to education in the matter of religion or belief in accordance with the wishes of his parents or, as the case may be, legal guardians, and shall not be compelled to receive teaching on religion or

---

270. Evans, C., *Freedom of Religion*, p. 89.
271. This construction was reinforced by the ECtHR in *Kjeldsen, Busk Madsen and Pedersen v. Denmark*, Application No. 5095/71; No. 5920/72; No. 5926/72, judgment of 7 December 1976, paragraph 50. See also Wildhaber, L., "Right to Education and Parental Rights", pp. 531-551, in R. St. J. Macdonald, F. Matscher and H. Petzold, eds., *The European System for the Protection of Human Rights*, Martinus Nijhoff, 1993, pp. 535, 550. Also Evans, C., *Freedom of Religion*, pp. 47-48, 89.
272. Evans, M., *Religious Liberty*, p. 356.
273. Proclaimed by General Assembly Resolution 1386(XIV) of 20 November 1959. See also Article 3.1 of the Convention on the Rights of the Child, G.A. res. 44/25, annex, 44 U.N. GAOR Supp. (No. 49), p. 167, U.N. Doc. A/44/49 (1989), entered into force 2 September 1990.

belief against the wishes of his parents or legal guardians, the best interests of the child being the guiding principle.²⁷⁴

Note, however, that action taken against parental choice in the best interest of the child requires state intervention,²⁷⁵ opening another opportunity for governmental intervention in matters of faith.

Constitutional provisions differ in defining the role of the state in religious education. After announcing the separation of religious associations and the state, the Macedonian Constitution declares that "the Macedonian Orthodox Church [as well as the Islamic Religious Community in Macedonia, the Catholic Church, Evangelic Methodist Church, Jewish Community] and other religious communities and groups are free to establish schools and other social and charitable institutions, by ways of a procedure regulated by law" (Article 19.4). The Constitution of Portugal also protects teaching as a manifestation of religious freedom (Article 41.5), at the same time it provides that public education shall be non-denominational (Article 43.3) and prohibits the state to "plan education and cultural development in accordance with any philosophical, aesthetic, political, ideological or religious precepts" (Article 43.2). In sharp contrast with this approach, the German Basic Law expressly provides for denominational education in public schools, as part of the regular curriculum (Article 7.3).²⁷⁶ This provision is supplemented via Article 140 with Article 137.1 of the Weimar Constitution saying that there shall be no state church. In constitutions which do not contain express provisions on religious education, guidance and inspiration may be taken from more general clauses on religious freedom, the right to education and church–state relations. Interestingly, as the foregoing analysis demonstrates, in cases on religious education, constitutional provisions on their own offer

---

274. Note that parental rights to organise family life are also protected in Article 5 of the Declaration.

275. See van Bueren, G., "The Right to be the Same the Right to be Different", pp. 561-570, in Lindholm, T., Durham, W.C. and Tahzib-Lie, B.G., eds, *Facilitating Freedom of Religion or Belief: A Deskbook*, Martinus Nijhoff, 2004.

276. Pursuant to the Basic Law's Bremen Clause (Article 141), this provision shall not apply in *Länder* in which *Land* law otherwise provided on 1 January 1949.

little guidance concerning the actual organisation of denominational education.

As a preliminary remark, it is also worth noting that in cases concerning the basic organisation of religious education, the requirement of equal treatment and non-discrimination is often interpreted with reference to such auxiliary considerations which leave certain religious communities at a clear disadvantage.[277] While constitutional courts appear willing to accommodate a wide variety of religious and non-religious beliefs upon individuals' claims for exemptions, in matters of education, states prefer to co-operate with registered or recognised religious associations. Among the latter, formerly established, traditional or majority churches enjoy a competitive advantage – a state of affairs which is often explained to honour the churches' historical contributions.[278] The Italian Constitutional Court for instance advised that "as a secular state, Italy provides instruction in the Catholic religion because of the formative value of a religious culture based on pluralism and because of the place of Catholic principles in the history of the Italian people" (Decision ITA-1989-R-001 a) Italy / b) Constitutional Court / c) / d) 11-04-1989 / e) 203/1989 / f) / g) *Gazzetta Ufficiale, Prima Serie Speciale* (Official Gazette), 16, 19.04.1989 / h) Codices (Italian)).

Denominational private schools

By definition, access to religious education does not entail a right to religious instruction in public schools. Furthermore, state funding

---

277. For example, when the Portuguese Constitutional Court reviewed the Concordat (concluded between Portugal and the Holy See in 1940) concerning the teaching of Catholic religion and moral standards in state schools the justices said it is not a violation of equal treatment that only Catholic religion classes are taught in public schools. Instead, the state committed a constitutional omission when it failed to provide the same treatment to other denominations (POR-1987-R-001 a) Portugal / b) Constitutional Court / c) Plenary / d) 27-10-1987 / e) 423/87 / f) / g) *Acordãos do Tribunal Constitucional* (Official Digest), Vol. 10, pp. 77-160 / h)) .

278. See, for example, HUN-1993-1-003 a) Hungary / b) Constitutional Court / c) / d) 27-02-1993 / e) 8/1993 / f) Church Case / g) *Magyar Közlöny* (Official Gazette), 22/1993 / h) Codices (Hungarian)). LTU-2000-2-006 a) Lithuania / b) Constitutional Court / c) / d) 13-06-2000 / e) 23/98 / f) On education / g) *Valstybes Zinios* (Official Gazette), 49-1424, 16.06.2000 / h) Codices (English).

for religious education in private schools does not automatically follow from religious freedom or from parental rights.[279] Despite the lack of constitutional obligation to this effect constitutional review fora do not reject government funding provided to private religious educational institutions. Public funding for denominational schools is available even in laïc France. Also, leaving the constitutional declaration of separation of churches and the state aside, the Hungarian Constitutional Court found in its leading decision on church–state relations that "while the state was to ensure the legal possibility of establishing non-neutral schools, it was not obliged to establish them. Where, however, the church or parents established or ran committed schools, the state was required to support them to the extent necessary to fulfil the state's obligations in them" (Decision HUN-1993-1-002 a) Hungary / b) Constitutional Court / c) / d) 12-02-1993 / e) 4/1993 / f) Church Property Case / g) *Magyar Közlöny* (Official Gazette), 15/1993 / h) Codices (Hungarian)). In a subsequent decision on education funding Hungarian constitutional justices added that "in addition to the compulsory budgetary contribution, the state or the local authority should provide schools owned by the church with additional financial assistance in proportion as these schools assume duties which would otherwise be carried out by the state or the local authority" (Decision HUN-1997-2-005 a) Hungary / b) Constitutional Court / c) / d) 25-04-1997 / e) 22/1997 / f) / g) *Magyar Közlöny* (Official Gazette), 35/1997 / h)). As a consequence, in Hungary, public schools as well as denominational private schools are funded by the state.[280]

---

279. See, for example, LIE-1996-R-001 a) Liechtenstein / b) State Council / c) / d) 24-05-1996 / e) StGH 1995/34 / f) / g) / h) *Liechtensteinische Entscheidsammlung 1997*, 78.
    For a similar conclusion from the Canadian Supreme Court see *Adler v. Ontario* [1996] 3 S.C.R. 609.
280. Note that according to the Italian Constitutional Court the state should provide all students with the same level of benefits irrespective of the type of school they attend, as "the provision of books free of charge is intended by law to benefit the pupils directly, rather than the schools, it is exclusively related to the actual obligation to attend school." (ITA-1994-3-019 a) Italy / b) Constitutional Court / c) / d) 15-12-1994 / e) 454/1994 / f) / g) *Gazzetta Ufficiale, Prima Serie Speciale* (Official Gazette), 1, 04.01.1995 / h) Codices (Italian)).

Governments may promote or limit the access to private religious education by means other than controlling funding. Granting or denying accreditation (recognition) to denominational schools or their certificates is more than a symbolic governmental gesture. As the Lichtenstein State Council explained, when licensing a private educational institution "in a pluralist society, there must also be room for private schools which adopted a very different educational or ideological approach; state control must therefore be confined to ensuring that the education they offered was basically equivalent" (Decision LIE-1996-R-001 Liechtenstein / b) State Council / c) / d) 24-05-1996 / e) StGH 1995/34 / f) / g) / h) *Liechtensteinische Entscheidsammlung 1997*, 78). Note that the accreditation process might provide an opportunity for a willing state to promote its value preferences in education. The Greek Council of States found that the admission of Orthodox students to a non-Orthodox denominational school was compatible with duty of the government to protect the Orthodox religion, provided that the state "may lay down conditions for the operation of such schools ... in order to preserve the religious identity of Orthodox pupils" (Decision GRE-1974-R-002 a) Greece / b) Council of State / c) Third Section / d) 29-06-1974 / e) 2349/74 / f) / g) / h)).

Religious education in public schools

Opinions in European legal systems differ greatly on how far a neutral state respecting freedom of religion and equality may go in providing room for religious education in public schools. According to the Macedonian Constitutional Court, state neutrality entails that public schools should be free from religious instruction (Decision MKD-2003-3-003 a) "The former Yugoslav Republic of Macedonia" / b) Constitutional Court / c) / d) 05-11-2003 / e) U.br. 42/2003 / f) / g) *Sluzben vesnik na Republika Makedonija* (Official Gazette), 73/2003 / h) Codices (Macedonian)).[281] In a similar logic, the Macedonian Constitutional Court found that a blessing

---

281. Interpreting a similar legal provision, the Slovenian Constitutional Court found that the state has "an obligation to permit (not to force, foster, support or even prescribe as mandatory) denominational activities in licensed kindergartens and schools outside public programmes financed from State funds." (SLO-2002-1-002 a) Slovenia / b) Constitutional Court / c) / d) 22-11-2001 / e) U-I-68/98 / f) / g) *Uradni list RS* (Official Gazette), 101/01 / h) Pravna praksa (abstract); Codices (English, Slovene)).

authorised by the Ministry of Education as a gesture for opening the school year violated religious freedom and the constitutional requirements of separation of church and state (Decision MKD-2000-1-002 a) "The former Yugoslav Republic of Macedonia" / b) Constitutional Court / c) / d) 19-04-2000 / e) U.br.195/99 / f) / g) *Sluzben vesnik na Republika Makedonija* (Official Gazette), 36/2000 / h) Codices (Macedonian)).[282]

Taking a milder approach, many European courts often conclude that state neutrality and co-operation between state and churches (or rather, one particular church) are compatible. The German state undertakes the financial burdens of religious instruction, while religious communities get to determine the contents of the courses offered.[283] Although this position seems to comply with the language of the Basic Law, other constitutional courts reached similar conclusions under constitutional provisions which call for more moderate state involvement or clear separation. The Portuguese Constitutional Court said, for instance, that the "state even has a responsibility to engage in such co-operation, in view of the positive dimension of religious freedom and its duty to co-operate with parents in the education of their children, but must do so within the limits imposed by the principles of state religious neutrality and non-denominational state education" (Decision POR-1993-1-007 a) Portugal / b) Constitutional Court / c) Plenary / d) 17-02-1993 / e) 174/93 / f) / g) *Acordãos do Tribunal Constitucional* (Official Digest), Vol. 24, 57-175 / h)).[284] The Polish Constitutional

---

282. The US Supreme Court is known for having taken a categorical stance prohibiting school prayers as a prohibition of establishment of religion under the First Amendment. *Engel v. Vitale*, 370 U.S. 421 (1962) on prohibiting a non-denominational school prayer, *Lee v. Weisman*, 505 U.S. 577 (1992), prohibiting non-denominational prayer at public school graduation and more recently *Santa Fe Independent School District v. Jane Doe*, 530 US 290 (2000), on school prayer before a school sports event in public schools.
In contrast, for example, according to the Polish Constitutional Tribunal, prayers in public schools do not "violate the constitutional provision prohibiting the forced participation (of school-children) in religious activities or rites (in so far as it is done upon the explicit request of school-children)" (POL-1993-2-009 a) Poland / b) Constitutional Tribunal / c) / d) 20-04-1993 / e) U 12/92 / f) / g) *Orzecznictwo Trybunalu Konstytucyjnego w 1993 roku* (Official Digest), 1993, Vol. 1, item 12 / h) Codices (Polish)).

283. Zacharias, "Access of Muslim Organizations to Religious Instruction", p. 1321.

284. The Constitutional Court was divided seven to six in the case.

Tribunal, in an early decision, also announced that religious classes taught in public schools by religious ministers were compatible with secularity and neutrality, as the rest of the curriculum in public schools did not contain religious aspects (Decision POL-1991-R-001 a) Poland / b) Constitutional Tribunal / c) / d) 30-01-1991 / e) K 11/90 / f) / g) *Orzecznictwo Trybunalu Konstytucyjnego w 1991 roku* (Official Digest), 1991, item 2 / h) Codices (Polish)).[285] Co-operation means more than allowing the teaching of a religion class in public schools: in Poland, as in many other cases, it entails state funding for educational projects supplied by religious associations in public schools.[286]

Control over the educational environment and the prohibition of indoctrination

In the United States, if permissible religious influence over public school curricula is mentioned, one is prompted to a tense public discourse over teaching evolution versus creationism.[287] Portrayals of sexuality and sex education in the public school curriculum also keep attracting considerable attention.[288] States differ in how much control they wish to retain over the public school curriculum.[289]

When setting a minimum standard in *Kjeldsen v. Denmark* – a case filed by parents seeking an exemption from mandatory sex education – the ECtHR said that:

---

285. For a commentary see Brzezinski, M., Garlicki, L., "Judicial Review in Post-Communist Poland. The Emergence of a Rechtsstaat?", 31, *Stanford Journal of International Law*, 13, 1995, pp. 48 et seq.

286. See, for example, POL-1993-2-009 a) Poland / b) Constitutional Tribunal / c) / d) 20-04-1993 / e) U 12/92 / f) / g) *Orzecznictwo Trybunalu Konstytucyjnego w 1993 roku* (Official Digest), 1993, Vol. 1, item 12 / h) Codices (Polish).

287. For an excellent summary see Dworkin, R., "Three Questions for America", 53 (14), *The New York Review of Books*, 21 September 2006. Also available at: http://www.nybooks.com/articles/19271.

288. For an analysis of pertinent jurisprudence see Adhar and Leigh, *Religious Freedom in the Liberal State*, pp. 252-255.

289. For an overview of national curricula on religious education/education about religion, see Plesner, I. T., "Promoting Tolerance through Religious Education", pp. 791-812, in Lindholm, T., Durham, C. W., Jr., Tahzib-Lie, B.G., eds, *Facilitating Freedom of Religion or Belief: A Deskbook*, Martinus Nijhoff, 2004.

the setting and planning of the curriculum fall in principle within the competence of the Contracting States ... In particular, the second sentence of Article 2 of the Protocol does not prevent States from imparting through teaching or education information or knowledge of a directly or indirectly religious or philosophical kind. It does not even permit parents to object to the integration of such teaching or education in the school curriculum, for otherwise all institutionalised teaching would run the risk of proving impracticable. ...

The second sentence of Article 2 implies on the other hand that the State, in fulfilling the functions assumed by it in regard to education and teaching, must take care that information or knowledge included in the curriculum is conveyed in an objective, critical and pluralistic manner. The State is forbidden to pursue an aim of indoctrination that might be considered as not respecting parents' religious and philosophical convictions. That is the limit that must not be exceeded.[290]

It is worth pointing out that these governing principles are understood to apply to the entire sphere of education, not restricted to teaching in class.[291] Compulsory religious instruction is acceptable under these standards, as long as it is objective and neutral, and does not indoctrinate in any particular manner.[292]

It will be interesting to see the application of these principles to mandatory religious instruction. In a case where the Norwegian Humanist Association challenged the mandatory "Christian Knowledge and Religious and Ethical Education" class, the Supreme Court of Norway – interpreting the standards stemming from ECtHR jurisprudence – said that the "requirement that the instruction should be objective, critical and pluralistic could not be interpreted in such a way that emphasis on the different world religions and philosophies of life must be distributed proportionally. It was acceptable that certain religions and philosophies were given a more dominant position than others, in the light of the history,

---

290. *Kjeldsen v. Denmark*, paragraph 53.
291. *Campbell and Cosans v. the United Kingdom*, Application Ns. 7511/76; No. 7743/76, judgment of 25 February 1982.
292. *Angelini v. Sweden*, Application No. 10491/83, 51 DR 41 paragraph 48 (1986).

culture and tradition of the individual member states" (Decision NOR-2001-2-005 a) Norway / b) Supreme Court / c) / d) 22-08-2001 / e) 2000/1533 / f) / g) *Norsk Retstidende* (Official Gazette), 2001, 1006 / h) Codices (Norwegian)). Further in the case, the Supreme Court refused to grant a full exemption from this mandatory class to children who wished to withdraw on grounds of conscience.[293]

The German understanding of state neutrality is compatible with most states having interdenominational schools of a Christian orientation. As the German Constitutional Court stated in the *School Prayer case*, the "state's power to shape the school system ... includes not only the power to organize the school structure but also (the power) to determine course content and objectives. Consequently, the state can pursue its own education goals in the classroom, goals which may be fundamentally independent of state aims."[294] According to the German Constitutional Court, in a secular educational environment it is possible to affirm Christianity not as a set of beliefs, but as a "formative cultural and educational factor", an approach which duly respects historical facts. "Confronting non-Christians with the view of the world in which the formative power of Christian thought is affirmed does not cause discrimination either against minorities not affiliated with Christianity or against their ideology."[295] In Gerhard Robbers' concise description of religious education in German public schools, "pupils belonging to a religious community for which

---

293. The ECtHR declared a challenge against this decision admissible in *Folgerø and Others v. Norway*, Application No. 15472/02 on 14 February, 2006.
Another case pending before the ECtHR concerning mandatory religious instruction is *Zengin v. Turkey*, Application No. 1448/04, declared admissible on 6 June 2006.

294. BVerfGE 52, 223. Available in English in Kommers, D. P., *The Constitutional Jurisprudence of the Federal Republic of Germany*, Duke, 1997, second edition, p. 462.

295. See "Interdenominational school case", in Kommers, *Constitutional Jurisprudence*, p. 470. Reaffirmed in the *School Prayer case*, BVerfGE 52, 223. Available in English in Kommers, *Constitutional Jurisprudence*, p. 463.
Compare with the Greek Council of State ruling that compulsory religious education in the teachings of Orthodox faith as a means of developing the "proper religious identity" of Greek children. This is the aim which parental rights in the sphere of education seek to achieve. As a consequence, the number of class hours devoted to religion classes shall not be reduced below a sufficient minimum (GRE-1998-R-001 a) Greece / b) Council of State / c) Sixth Section / d) 26-05-1998 / e) 2176/98 / f) / g) / h).

religious instruction is offered, have to participate. They can opt out of those classes. Often but not always – depending on the specific *Land* – they and the other pupils not belonging to any of those communities have to take part in courses of ethics, instead."[296]

The right to be exempted from religious activities

So far the section analysed the institutional aspects of denominational education and the focus was on legal measures adopted by various states to promote religious freedom. Instances where freedom of conscience as an individual right sets the limit to state action in the sphere of religious education most often claim for an exemption from religious activities. Such exemptions are permitted even in countries where religious education is otherwise mandatory.[297] The justification for seeking such an exemption rests on the prohibition of coercion in matters of faith. Furthermore, it is worth noting that the European exemption cases typically deal with exemptions from religious classes or activities and not with requests for exemption from public schooling altogether, and rarely raise concerns about religious secessionism.[298] Nonetheless, claims which are filed by members of disliked or unacknowledged religious communities are often perceived by national authorities as threats to a polity's identity or even to national sovereignty.[299]

---

296. Robbers, G., "Country Report, The Federal Republic of Germany, on School-Religion Relations", at p. 11, available at: http://www.strasbourgconference.org/papers/On%20School%20Religion%20Relations.pdf.
Compare with the Italian Constitutional Court finding that there is no need to prescribe an ethics class for those students who request to be exempted from the Catholic religion class (ITA-1989-R-001 a) Italy / b) Constitutional Court / c) / d) 11-04-1989 / e) 203/1989 / f) / g) *Gazzetta Ufficiale, Prima Serie Speciale* (Official Gazette), 16, 19.04.1989 / h) Codices (Italian)).

297. CYP-1994-R-001 a) Cyprus / b) Supreme Court / c) / d) 21-04-1994 / e) 501 / f) *Arvanitakis and Others v. Republic of Cyprus* / g) 1994, 4 Cyprus Law Reports (Official Digest), 859 / h). (Being a Jehovah's Witness qualifies as a special reason and may be a ground for such an exemption)

298. *Wisconsin v. Yoder*, 406 US 205 (1972). Compare with *Board of Education of Kiryas Joel Village School District v. Grumet*, 512 US 687 (1994). See Dorsen, *Comparative Constitutionalism*, pp. 1019-1020.

299. In this respect it is worth following the struggle of Alevis in Turkey to be exempted from mandatory religious instruction in a case which was found admissible by the ECtHR. See *Zengin v. Turkey*, Application No. 1448/04, declared admissible on 6 June 2006.

In general, European constitutional courts acknowledge that students should be exempted from religion classes and other religious activities on grounds of conscience. Although it is widely acknowledged in European constitutional jurisprudence that the prohibition of compulsion in matters of faith requires states to exempt pupils from religious activities,[300] courts differ in what amounts to compulsion in an education environment. In part, such hesitation results from the difficulty to distinguish in a principled manner between the *forum internum* and external manifestations of religion. Note that the ECtHR's sensitivity towards coercion in an education environment is regrettably low. In *Valsamis v. Greece*,[301] the ECtHR held that suspending a student who refused on grounds of conscience to attend a parade on an official holiday commemorating the outbreak of war between Greece and Fascist Italy on 28 October 1940 did not violate convention rights. The student was a Jehovah's Witness who claimed that a commemoration of a war was against her religion. The ECtHR said that the purpose as well as the arrangement of the parade was compatible with pacifist beliefs. In assessing the intensity of coercion, the justices took note of the fact that the student was otherwise regularly exempted from Orthodox religious instruction and mass. It is believed that the search for indoctrination – which is customary in education cases – diverted the ECtHR's attention from the problem of coercion.[302]

When granting such exemptions, courts are often required to assess not only if joining a school prayer is coercive, but also whether the precondition of receiving an exemption (which very often entails revealing one's faith or the lack thereof) or the circumstances which the student is to face once an exemption is granted are such as to infringe religious freedom. The Greek Council of State ruled that once a student requested an exemption, the school is required to take action immediately. Furthermore, students who were exempted from man-

---

300. For example, ROM-1995-2-003 a) Romania / b) Constitutional Court / c) / d) 18-07-1995 / e) 72/1995 / f) / g) *Monitorul Oficial al României* (Official Gazette), 167/31.07.1995; Curtea Constitutionala, *Culegere de decizii si hotarâri 1995* (Official Digest), 106, 1995 / h) .
301. *Valsamis v. Greece*, Application No. 21787/93, judgment of 18 December 1996.
302. Plesner, I. T., "Legal Limitations to Freedom of Religion or Belief in School Education", 19, *Emory International Law Review*, 557, 2005, pp. 571-572.

datory religious instruction were not supposed to be subjected to punishment (Decision GRE-1995-2-001 a) Greece / b) Council of State / c) Sixth Section / d) 19-06-1995 / e) 3356/95 / f) / g) / h)). The German Constitutional Court also found the voluntary, non-denominational prayers in interdenominational public schools compatible with the Basic Law, provided that students who did not wish to participate had a meaningful way to be exempted from such prayers. When it comes to optional school prayers, the role of the state is restricted to create a setting where a school prayer may take place on the initiative of parents or pupils (Decision GER-1979-R-001 a) Germany / b) Federal Constitutional Court / c) First Panel / d) 16-10-1979 / e) 1 BvR 647/70, 7/74 / f) / g) *Entscheidungen des Bundesverfassungsgerichts* (Official Digest), 52, 223 / h)).

Religious symbols in school: The limits of religious tolerance and pluralism

The prohibition of coercion and religious indoctrination goes beyond questions of designing the curriculum and the number of class hours devoted to religious instruction. The question whether religious symbols shall be permitted in classrooms in public schools appeared before many constitutional review fora in Europe. While the Polish Constitutional Court does not find the display of crucifixes in schools problematic,[303] the Swiss Federal Court found that it violates state neutrality.[304] In its famous decision on the display of crucifixes in Bavarian public school classrooms, the German

---

[303.] POL-1993-2-009. (a) Poland; (b) Constitutional Tribunal; (c); (d) 20-04-1993; (e) U 12/92; (f); (g) *Orzecznictwo Trybunalu Konstytucyjnego w 1993 roku* (Official Digest), 1993, Vol. 1, item 12; (h) Codices (Polish).
In 2004, the Italian Constitutional Court left untouched a Fascist-era law prescribing the display of crosses in public school classrooms due to the procedural imperfections in the case, *Ordinanza*, 389/2004. An English translation of the decision is available at the Italian Constitutional Court's website via: http://www.cortecostituzionale.it/eng/attivitacorte/pronunceemassime/abstract/abstract_2004.asp. A heated debate over crucifixes in classrooms, courtrooms and public hospitals persists. See *Italy, International Religious Freedom Report 2006*, available at: http://www.state.gov/g/drl/rls/irf/2006/71387.htm.

[304.] SUI-1990-R-001. (a) Switzerland; (b) Federal Court; (c) First public law Chamber; (d) 26-09-1990; (e) 1P.675/1989; (f) *Cadro v. Guido Bernasconi and the Administrative Court of the Canton of Ticino*; (g) *Arrêts du Tribunal fédéral* (Official Digest), 116 Ia 252; (h) Codices (Italian).

Constitutional Court[305] started from the premise that while in a multi-religious society individuals do not have a right not to be exposed to symbols of religions other than their own, this does not empower the state to expose individuals to religious symbols. The justices stated that in a multi-religious polity, a neutral state is a guarantor of peaceful co-existence. In the analysis, the Constitutional Court said that:

> [the cross] symbolises man's redemption from the original sin through Christ's sacrifice just as it represents Christ's victory over Satan and death and his powers over the world. .... To this day, the presence of a cross in a home or room is understood as an expression of the dweller's Christian faith. On the other hand, because of the significance Christianity attributes to the cross, non-Christians and atheists perceive it to be the symbolic expression of certain faith convictions and a symbol of missionary zeal. To see the cross as nothing more than a cultural artefact of the Western tradition without any particular religious meaning would amount to a profanation contrary to the self-understanding of Christians and the Christian church.[306]

According to the Constitutional Court, the degree of compulsion triggered by a crucifix in a classroom is such that it cannot be mounted on the classroom walls of public schools in a neutral state.[307] In this case, the Constitutional Court reinforced its stance that state neutrality is compatible with a Christian orientation in public education, saying that "Christianity as a cultural force incorporates in particular the idea of tolerance towards people of different persuasions. Confrontation with a Christian world view will not lead to

---

305. GER-1995-2-019 a) Germany / b) Federal Constitutional Court / c) First Panel / d) 16-05-1995 / e) 1 BvR 1087/91 / f) / g) *Entscheidungen des Bundesverfassungsgerichts* (Official Digest), 93, 1 / h) *Europäische Grundrechte Zeitschrift*, 1995, 359; *Neue Juristische Wochenschrift*, 1995, 2477; Codices (German).

306. *Classroom Crucifix II*, BVErfGE 93, 1, in English in Kommers, *Constitutional Jurisprudence*, p. 475.

307. See also GER-1973-R001 a) Germany / b) Federal Constitutional Court / c) First Panel / d) 17-07-1973 / e) 1 BvR 308/69 / f) / g) *Entscheidungen des Bundesverfassungsgerichts* (Official Digest), 35, 366 / h) wherein the Federal Constitutional Court refused to say that the display of a crucifix in a courtroom was *per se* unconstitutional, although the justices acknowledged that it might violate fundamental rights.

discrimination or devaluation of a non-Christian ideology so long as the state does not impose the values of the Christian faith on non-Christians."[308]

The crucifix cases became the foyer of a much more spectacular conundrum surrounding students and teachers wearing an Islamic headscarf in public schools. The headscarf issue started out small, with a few cases where female Muslim students were exempted from swimming lessons.[309] A round of serious controversy arose in France out of a case where three female students were expelled from a secondary school after refusing to remove their headscarf. The Council of State ruled that a headscarf could be worn in neutral French public schools as long as it did not amount to religious propaganda within the school, did not obstruct ordinary school operation or did not otherwise violate public order within the school.[310] Currently the limelight is shared by the 2004 French law banning students in public schools from wearing religious symbols,[311] the *Leyla Sahin v. Turkey* decision,[312] wherein the ECtHR upheld Turkey's ban on students' headscarves on university premises, and the flood of German state (*Land*) laws banning public school teachers from wearing headscarves (and sometimes other

---

308. *Classroom Crucifix II decision*, available in Kommers, *Constitutional Jurisprudence*, p. 477.
309. SUI-1993-3-008 a) Switzerland / b) Federal Court / c) Second public law Chamber / d) 18-06-1993 / e) 2P.292/1992 / f) *M. v. Council of State of the Canton of Zurich* / g) *Arrêts du Tribunal fédéral* (Official Digest), 119 Ia 178 / h) *Semaine judiciaire*, 1994, 43; *Zentralblatt für Staats- und Verwaltungsrecht*, 95, 1994, 24; *Europäische Grundrechte Zeitschrift*, 1993, 400; Codices (German). For a similar decision from the German Federal Administrative Court see BVerwGE 94, 82.
310. Avis n° 346.893 - 27 novembre 1989, available in French at: http://www.conseil-etat.fr/ce/missio/index_mi_cg03_01.shtml. For a discussion in English, see Troper, M., "The Problem of the Islamic Veil", pp. 89-102, in Sajó, A. and Avineri, Sh., eds, *The Law of Religious Identity, Models for Post-Communism*, Kluwer, 1999. Also, Beller, E. T., "The Headscarf Affair, The Conseil d'Etat on the Role of Religion and Culture in French Society", 39, *Texas International Law Journal*, 581, 2004.
311. Loi n° 2004-228 du 15 mars 2004 encadrant, en application du principe de laïcité, le port de signes ou de tenues manifestant une appartenance religieuse dans les écoles, collèges et lycées. The act amends the Education Code.
312. *Leyla Sahin v. Turkey*, Application No. 44774/98, judgment of 29 June 2004.

religious symbols), bans which were enacted in response to the German Federal Constitutional Court's decision in 2003.[313]

The French ban was enacted in a tense political atmosphere, marked by growing unease about new religious movements and Islam, in which numerous governmental investigations and agencies were established.[314] A most influential body among these, the Stasi Commission, explained in 2003 the symbolic significance of the Islamic headscarf in the following terms:

> For those wearing it, the veil can have various significances. It can be a personal choice or on the contrary a constraint, particularly intolerable for young people ... For those not wearing it, the significance of the Islamic veil stigmatizes "the pubescent girl or the woman like a lone person in charge for the desire for the man", a sight which is in basic contravention with the principle of equality of men and women. For the school community, too often the wearing of the veil causes suffering and division, even conflict. Many feel that the display of a religious symbol is against the mission of the school which must be a space of neutrality and a place of awakening of the critical mind.[315]

As a reaction, the French Parliament adopted a ban on religious symbols in public schools in order to protect the secularity (*laïcité*) of public education.

While the French political forces attracted much criticism with introducing this ban, the 2004 French law seems to comply with the subsequent decision of the ECtHR in the *Leyla Sahin v. Turkey* case. In this case, the ECtHR accepted the Turkish Constitutional Court's position, holding that the ban on headscarves worn on university premises was required by secularism. Furthermore, the ECtHR added (para 98) that:

---

313. For an English-language description of these laws, see, for example, Langenfled, C., and Moshen, S., "Germany: The Teacher Headscarf Case," 3, *International Journal of Constitutional Law*, 86, 2005, p. 90, Robbers, "Freedom of Religion or Belief in Germany", 2005, pp. 881-882.
314. See also Section 4.2.
315. "Le Rapport de la Commission Stasi sur la laïcité", *Le Monde*, 12 December 2003, p. 17.

in the decisions of *Karaduman v. Turkey* and *Dahlab v. Switzerland* the Convention institutions found that in a democratic society the State was entitled to place restrictions on the wearing of the Islamic headscarf if it was incompatible with the pursued aim of protecting the rights and freedoms of others, public order and public safety. In the *Dahlab* case ... [the EctHR] stressed among other matters the impact that the "powerful external symbol" conveyed by her wearing a headscarf could have and questioned whether it might have some kind of proselytising effect, seeing that it appeared to be imposed on women by a precept laid down in the Koran that was hard to reconcile with the principle of gender equality.

Unlike the cases discussed so far, the decision of the German Constitutional Court in the teacher's headscarf case (also known as the Ludin case) affected not the rights of students, but those of teachers. The public authorities of the German state (*Land*) of Baden-Württemberg found the applicant unfit for becoming a school teacher because she refused to give up wearing an Islamic headscarf.[316] Although acknowledging that religious freedom encompassed the wearing of the headscarf, the case was decided on a rather narrow, technical ground, namely, the lack of statutory framework underlying the decision of the state authority to impose a ban on religious garb.[317] The Constitutional Court said that it was the duty of state legislatures to create an appropriate legislative regulation on the matter, although the constitutional justices were silent about the standard to be introduced.

While there is no room for a detailed analysis of these decisions in the framework of the current analysis, there are a few themes which are worth noting even briefly. In the above cases there is a strong emphasis on the peculiar understanding of the states' stance

---

316. GER-2003-3-018 a) Germany / b) Federal Constitutional Court / c) Second Panel / d) 03-06-2003 / e) 2 BvR 1436/02 / f) / g) / h) *Neue Juristische Wochenschrift* 2003, 3111-3118; *Europäische Grundrechte Zeitschrift 2003*, 621-628; Codices (German).
For the procedural of the history summarised in English, see Frhr. von Campenhausen, A., "The German Headscarf Debate", 2004, *Brigham Young University Law Review*, 665, 2004, pp. 672-677.

317. See Eberle, E. J., "Free Exercise of Religion in Germany and the United States", 78, *Tulane Law Review* 1023, 2004, p. 1064.

towards religion, may that be called state neutrality (Germany), *laïcité* (France) or secularity (Turkey). In contrast, it is striking how little emphasis the courts in these cases placed on the fact that the wearing of a headscarf is a manifestation of the religious freedom of the Muslim women whose rights are at issue in the given cases.[318] Instead, the courts and the report keep focusing on the Islamic headscarf as a symbol.[319] In most examples, the headscarf is not understood as a religious symbol, but as a primarily political one, being the reminder of subjection of women or even of Islam fundamentalism (*Karaduman v. Turkey*). When the religious implications of the headscarf are acknowledged, it is in the form of a conclusion that it has a potentially proselytising effect to be taken into account. Certainly, the assessment of symbols (religious or secular) is not a trivial task. In this process, one has to be mindful of the symbolic effect of a legislative or judicial ban on a particular religious insignia. As the Canadian Supreme Court acknowledged recently in a case which involved a ban on a ritual dagger of Sikh students that "a total prohibition against wearing a kirpan to school undermines the value of this religious symbol and sends students the message that some religious practices do not merit the same protection as others."[320]

Thus, the headscarf is being taken as a source of danger at large, especially when worn in an educational environment. When reflecting on the facts of the actual case, the German Constitutional Court said that:

> The school authority and the non-constitutional courts present the view that the complainant's intention to wear a headscarf while teaching at school constitutes a lack of aptitude because pre-emptive action should be taken against possible influence on the pupils, and conflicts, which cannot be ruled

---

318. This point is made with regard to the various ECtHR decisions in Evans, C. "The 'Islamic Scarf' in the European Court of Human Rights", 7, *Melbourne Journal of International Law*, 52, 2006, p. 55.
319. Compare with the Swiss federal court in the *Dahlab* case characterising the issue as the "wearing of a powerful religious symbol by a teacher at a State school in the performance of her professional duties." As quoted in *Dahlab v. Switzerland*. *Dahlab v. Switzerland*, Application No. 42393/98, ECHR 2001-V.
320. *Multani v. Commission scolaire Marguerite-Bourgeoys* [2006] 1 S.C.R. 256, 2006 SCC 6, paragraph 79.

out, between teachers and pupils or their parents should be avoided in advance ... No tangible evidence could be seen in the proceedings before the non-constitutional courts that the complainant's appearance when wearing a headscarf created a concrete danger to the peace at school. The fear that conflicts might arise with parents who object to their children being taught by a teacher wearing a headscarf cannot be substantiated by experience of the complainant's previous teaching as a trainee.

Nonetheless, even the German justices were unwilling to say that the headscarf does not constitute a "danger" *per se*.[321]

This is all the more unfortunate as arguments in favour of banning religious symbols from public schools are heavy with concern for the coercive impact of religious symbols in an education environment. Public education is often said to be a unique sphere where impressions are made on all participants under special conditions, although in European courts no conclusive evidence was submitted on the impact of religious symbols on students' development. Note, however, that religious symbols worn by teachers are believed to be different from the ones displayed on students not so much because of the different impact these symbols might have on students, but owing to the fact that teachers in public schools are public (i.e. state) employees. The dissenters in the German teacher headscarf decision focused on the fact that public school teachers are public servants, noting that a "civil servant's particular position of duty takes precedence over the protection of the fundamental rights, which in principle applies to civil servants too, to the extent that the duty and purpose of the public office so

---

321. Gerstenberg, O. "Germany: Freedom of Conscience in Public Schools", 3, *International Journal of Constitutional Law*, 94, 2005, p. 96, suggests that the notion of danger should be understood in the light of the fact that – in addition to freedom of conscience – the German Constitutional Court considers "Christian culture" as value-defining German political identity and a factor on which the German polity's cohesion is based.

require."[322] This argument is familiar from the cases involving the observance of religious holidays, wherein many courts insisted that religious employers entered into employment contracts limiting their religious freedom upon their free will.[323] Courts are noticeably unwilling to acknowledge the impact such basic choices concerning employment might have on religious freedom.[324]

Analysis of the headscarf as a symbol is often dominated by the audiences' perspective and perception, leaving the believer (the applicant) behind and allowing very little room for analysing the Islamic headscarf as a manifestation of religious freedom and considering potential solutions for accommodation. Under the current approach, governmental actors and courts retain such monopolies of interpretation which do not allow for a sensitive assessment of particular applicants' claims. As a result, many arguments shift to a plain where they undermine the applicants' cases rather than foster a sensitive evaluation. Note, for instance, that in other cases where accommodation is requested in order to create room for free exercise, European courts were seen to provide protection to

---

322. Compare with the Spanish Constitutional Court saying that, "It is therefore the very nature of the professional service performed by teachers in educational institutions which makes it necessary to balance their pedagogical freedom against the school's freedom to lay down its own ideology" (ESP-1996-2-018. (a) Spain; (b) Constitutional Court; (c) Second Chamber; (d) 12-06-1996; (e) 106/1996; (f); (g) *Boletín oficial del Estado* (Official Gazette), 168, 12.07.1996, pp. 37-43; (h)).
See also the decision of the Greek Council of State finding that a Jehovah's Witness may be appointed as a philology teacher in a secondary school because he does not influence students' development of religious identity (GRE-1986-R-001 (a) Greece; (b) Council of State; (c) Third Section; (d) 24-07-1986; (e) 3533/86; (f); (g); (h)).

323. See Section 2.2 for further details. Note that similar arguments are routinely raised against the free exercise claims of private-sector employees who wish to wear religious symbols at their workplace.

324. Compare with, according to the Greek Council of State, legislative or administrative restrictions which required Orthodox ministers to abandon the clergy if they wished to become teachers in public schools trigger an unacceptable "crisis of conscience" and are therefore unconstitutional (GRE-1983-R-001. (a) Greece; (b) Council of State; (c) Third Section; (d) 20-10-1983; (e) 4045/83; (f); (g); (h)). In the Greek case, the prohibition on Orthodox ministers (who receive their salary from the state) to serve simultaneously as teachers in public school was introduced to prevent teacher-priests to take a second salary from the state.

such behaviour explained to be motivated by individual conviction which was otherwise not required by the doctrines of a particular approach. In contrast, in cases involving an Islamic headscarf, arguments that a headscarf is not required by religious doctrine but is a mere custom, tend to undermine the applicants' case, thus visibly narrowing their religious freedom.

Similarly, legislators and courts banning an Islamic headscarf from public schools with reference to a state's commitment to pluralism are rarely seen to consider the consequences of the ban. Indeed, students who are barred from wearing their head coverings are very likely to move to private schools, which do not follow the state's educational mission. The Canadian Supreme Court in the Multani case found that the very fact that the Sikh student who was prohibited from wearing his ritual dagger left the public school system and attended a private school contributed to the infringement of his religious freedom.[325] Unfortunately, without a more sensitive judicial strategy, which is willing to look behind the veil and enquire into applicants' actual cases and petitioners, European democracies remain trapped between secularisation and multiculturalism.[326]

3.3. Accommodation in prisons and military establishments

Prisons[327] and military[328] environments present special problems for advocates of religious freedom. In such highly regulated and restricted environments the exercise of many fundamental rights is limited.[329] It is widely accepted that in such establishments, religious freedom cannot be exercised, unless the government is will-

---

325. *Multani v. Commission scolaire Marguerite-Bourgeoys*, paragraph 40.
326. Schlink, B., "Between Secularisation and Multiculturalism", pp. 77-88, in Sajó, A. and Avineri, S., eds, *The Law of Religious Identity, Models for Post-Communism*, Kluwer, 1999, p. 80.
327. The term "prison" is used in a broad sense, encompassing all forms of detention (including pre-trial detention).
328. Cases concerning access to and restrictions on religious freedom in the military are relevant not only in jurisdictions where military service is still compulsory, but also for countries with a volunteer army. Rights of conscientious objectors were treated in Section 2.4.
329. The section does not address difficulties with the exercise of other fundamental rights.

ing to undertake positive measures to accommodate believers and facilitate their free exercise. Such positive measures are believed to be appropriate even in neutral and secular states, although the extent to which the government is bound to undertake accommodation is often unclear.

Difficulties arise from the fact that the requirements of military and prison discipline might often clash with basic premises of the exercise of religious freedom. Furthermore, exactly due to the unique nature of these environments, courts and commentators are willing to accept a remarkably wide array of justifications for restricting the religious freedom of prisoners and military personnel.[330] Much caution is reflected in the language of General Comment No. 22, saying that "Persons already subject to certain legitimate constraints, such as prisoners, continue to enjoy their rights to manifest their religion or belief to the fullest extent compatible with the specific nature of the constraint."[331] As an additional problem, measures of accommodation often benefit majority or dominant faiths (and registered religious organisations), and leave out minority and new religions, a consequence which furthers inequalities between believers and religious communities

> *Case law*
>
> - AUT-1985-R-001 a) Austria / b) Constitutional Court / c) / d) 27-09-1985 / e) B 643/82 / f) / g) *Erkenntnisse und Beschlüsse des Verfassungsgerichtshofes* (Official Digest), 10547/1985 of 27.09.1985 / h) .
>
> The applicant, a practising Jew, had been arrested by the police (because he was suspected of an offence). While he was in custody, the police authorities refused to give him a phylactery and a prayer shawl; thus, he could not use them in order to pray.
>
> The Constitutional Court ruled that this constituted a violation of the prisoner's religious freedom. Article 14 of the Basic Law of the State (StGG) and Article 9, ECHR, guaranteed each individual the right to choose his or her religion

---

330. Evans, C., *Freedom of Religion*, p. 151.
331. *General Comment No. 22*, paragraph 8.

freely without interference from the state, and to engage in religious activities in accordance with his or her beliefs. Essentially, this fundamental right prohibited the state from imposing constraints in relation to religion. Every individual must enjoy absolute, unlimited freedom in denominational and religious matters.

...

- SUI-2003-1-004 a) Switzerland / b) Federal Court / c) Second Public Law Chamber / d) 13-01-2003 / e) 2P.245/2002, 2P.246/2002 / f) X. v. Sentence Enforcement Office and Ministry of Justice and Home Affairs of the Canton of Zurich / g) *Arrêts du Tribunal fédéral suisse* (Official Digest), 129 I 74 / h) Codices (German).

...

X asked to attend the Orthodox Church Easter ceremony that was to be held in the worship and meditation area of the prison's social centre. Given the conditions of X's imprisonment, the prison governor turned down his request. He offered a visit by a clergyman, which, owing to misunderstandings, did not take place ...

Subsequently, X refused to work in the prison on certain days on the grounds that those days were official Orthodox religious holidays devoted to prayer. Because of that refusal, X had been subject to disciplinary measures taken by the prison governor. His appeal to the Ministry of Justice and Home Affairs was dismissed. X responded by lodging a second Constitutional complaint asking the Federal Court to set aside the decision of the Ministry of Justice and Home Affairs.

The Federal Court dismissed both complaints. Regarding the first, the Federal Court found that freedom of worship formed part of freedom of religion and conscience within the meaning of Article 15 of the Federal Constitution, the European Convention on Human Rights and the UN International Covenant on Civil and Political Rights. Prisoners may invoke freedom of religion and conscience while serving their sentences. The authorities must ensure that prisoners can attend religious services. However, that freedom is not absolute and may be restricted. To comply with the Constitution, the restrictions must have an adequate legal basis, be justified by an overriding public interest and satisfy the proportionality principle.

... A legal basis existed not only for deprivation of freedom as such but also for the isolation of prisoners likely to abscond and presenting a risk to prison staff and other prisoners. Sentence enforcement and the proper functioning of prison life demand certain restrictions, including freedom of worship. Account may be taken of the danger that the defendant will abscond and of the need for isolation.

The exclusion from corporate worship cannot be considered disproportionate. The applicant could have had a visit from a clergyman and did not risk being expelled from the Orthodox Church for having failed to take part in the Easter celebration.

Regarding the second constitutional complaint, the Federal Court noted that freedom of religion and conscience also covered observance of religious holidays. Under the relevant provisions, prisoners are required to perform the work allocated to them. To guarantee the smooth running of the prison and ensure calm among its 400 prisoners, the latter are not free to choose the days on which they will be exempted from work on religious grounds. The Orthodox religion did not prohibit work on the holidays cited. The applicant could request pastoral care from a clergyman and devote himself to prayer outside working hours. The obligation to work on those days as well did not ultimately seem either disproportionate or contrary to the principle of equal treatment. It could not be compared to the release of Muslim prisoners for weekly prayers on Friday evenings and bore no relation to the general exemption from school on Saturdays for religious reasons.

Commentary

Basic theoretical and practical problems with accommodation in restricted environments

In a well-known decision in *Goldman v. Weinberger* the US Supreme Court rejected a complaint by a Jewish army officer who sought to wear his yarmulke, due to the following reasons:

The military need not encourage debate or tolerate protest to the extent that such tolerance is required of the civilian state by the First Amendment; to accomplish its mission the military must foster instinctive obedience, unity, commitment, and esprit de corps. ... When evaluating whether military needs justify a particular restriction on religiously motivated conduct, courts must give great deference to the professional judgment of military authorities concerning the relative importance of a particular military interest ... [The First Amendment] does not require the military to accommodate such practices in the face of its view that they would detract from the uniformity sought by the dress regulations.[332]

In response to the Supreme Court, Congress enacted legislation which provides that "a member of the armed forces may wear an item of religious apparel while wearing the uniform," unless "the wearing of the item would interfere with the performance [of] military duties [or] the item of apparel is not neat and conservative."[333] Recently in *Cutter v. Wilkinson*,[334] a unanimous Supreme Court upheld a federal statute providing for the governmental accommodation of religious freedom in prison (without finding a violation of the First Amendment's Establishment Clause). The relevant parts of Section 3 of the Religious Land Use and Institutionalized Persons Act of 2000 (RLUIPA),[335] provides that "No government shall impose a substantial burden on the religious exercise of a person residing in or confined to an institution", unless the burden furthers "a compelling governmental interest", and does so by "the least restrictive means."

The need for positive governmental measures to facilitate exercise of religious freedom in prisons and military establishments is widely

---

332. *Goldman v. Weinberger*, 475 US 503 (1986), 506-510.
333. 10 U. S. C. §774(a)-(b).
334. *Cutter v. Wilkinson*, 544 US 709 (2005).
335. 114 Stat. 804, 42 U. S. C. paragraph 2000cc-1(a)(1)-(2).

acknowledged in European democracies.[336] Recommendation No. R (87) 3 of the rules[337] provides:

> 46. So far as practicable, every prisoner shall be allowed to satisfy the needs of his religious, spiritual and moral life by attending the services or meetings provided in the institution and having in his possession any necessary books or literature.
>
> 47. 1. If the institution contains a sufficient number of prisoners of the same religion, a qualified representative of that religion shall be appointed and approved. If the number of prisoners justifies it and conditions permit, the arrangement should be on a full-time basis.
>
> 2. A qualified representative appointed or approved under paragraph 1 shall be allowed to hold regular services and activities and to pay pastoral visits in private to prisoners of his religion at proper times.
>
> 3. Access to a qualified representative of any religion shall not be refused to any prisoner. If any prisoner should object to a visit of any religious representative, the prisoner shall be allowed to refuse it.

The potential for tensions between requirements of state neutrality and accommodation of religious freedom in prisons and within the armed forces is prevalent.[338] Despite this apparent tension, commentators agree that the exercise of religious freedom in

---

336. The Austrian Constitutional Court was much criticised when it concluded in 1975 that "It is legitimate to prevent a remand prisoner from attending a religious service held in prison. This does not violate religious freedom (Article 14 of the Basic Law of the State of 1867 and Article 9 ECHR). The republic is not obliged to take special measures to enable legally detained persons to exercise this individual right." AUT-1972-R-001 a) Austria / b) Constitutional Court / c) / d) 20-06-1972 / e) B 223/69 / f) / g) *Erkenntnisse und Beschlüsse des Verfassungsgerichtshofes* (Official Digest), 6747/1972 of 20.06.1972 / h).

337. Adopted by the Committee of Ministers on 12 February 1987 at the 404th meeting of the Ministers' Deputies.

338. See, for example, "Le Rapport de la Commission Stasi sur la laïcite," *Le Monde*, 12 December 2003, pp. 17-18. Note that in France the legal framework establishing the army chaplaincy predates the 1905 act. See Act of 8 July 1880 on the invalidity of the Act of 20 May-3 June 1874 on the Army Chaplaincy (BL XXI, No. 546, p. 138).

restricted environments, such as in the armed forces and in prisons, is not possible without positive state action.[339] Among the manifestations of religious freedom which are dependent on relatively wide-scale accommodation measures, one may find access to pastoral services, attendance of religious services and the observation of religious dietary regimes. There is no agreement on the proper nature and extent of necessary accommodation of religious exercise. In several European states, statutory frameworks establish some form of a chaplaincy for the army and prisons. As a supplement or alternative to a statutory scheme, bilateral agreements (concordats and treaties) between the affected churches and the state establish the terms of such pastoral services for both the armed forces and detention facilities.[340]

Problems mentioned before on account of national legal solutions for registering religious organisations are well illustrated in the specific context of prisons and the armed forces: religious communities which are not registered or recognised otherwise in a state are at an apparent disadvantage in gaining access to penitentiaries and facilities of the armed forces. As was pointed out, due to lack of centralisation in their religious organisations, Muslim communities are facing difficulties with accessing any legal solution access to which is ensured via a recognised representative organisation. In order to alleviate such difficulties in Germany, "Ministry of Defense efforts to develop a Muslim chaplaincy have failed because of an inability to reach agreement on a plan with the multiple Muslim groups. Independently, the ministry has developed a code of conduct to facilitate the practice of Islam by an estimated 3 000 Muslim soldiers."[341]

Note that the Hungarian Constitutional Court sanctioned a clear differentiation among registered religious organisations in a case

---

339. For example, Dufaux, J., et al., *Liberté religieuse et régimes des cultes en droit francais* (CERF, 2005), p. 1153.
340. See, for example, Iban, I. C., "State and Church in Spain", pp. 94-117, in Robbers, G., ed., *State and Church in the European Union*, Nomos, 1996, pp. 112 et seq. and Ferrari, S., "Church and State in Italy", pp. 169-190, in:Robbers, G., ed., *State and Church in the European Union*, Nomos, 1996, pp. 184 and seq.
341. *Germany, International Religious Freedom Report 2006*, at: http://www.state.gov/g/drl/rls/irf/2006/71382.htm.

where petitioners challenged the Cabinet decree on the Army Chaplaincy which requires the chaplains to come from four specified denominations (Roman Catholic, Reformed, Evangelical and Jewish). The preamble of the Cabinet decree explains that the Chaplaincy was established in this particular manner upon agreements concluded by the government and these "historic churches".[342] In its decision[343] upholding the decree, the Constitutional Court was satisfied with seeing that the establishment of the Chaplaincy was preceded by a voluntary opinion poll in the armed forces concerning religious affiliation. Constitutional justices were not bothered by the reference to "historic churches" either, remarking that the phrase stands for the historical record proper. According to the Constitutional Court, the singling out of these particular denominations does not constitute unconstitutional discrimination or any other violation of freedom of religion. Subsequently, a Chaplaincy was established along similar lines for prisons.[344] (It is not much consolation, if any, that in youth disciplinary facilities minors shall have access to support and guidance of a representative of any religion of their choice, and communication with such a religious advise shall be unsupervised.[345])

It is important to point out that in restricted environments, and especially in prisons, accommodation of the needs of believers does not halt at providing an opportunity for allowing religious services on prison premises. In this respect the decision of the Swiss Federal Court is sobering, as it clearly demonstrates how the organisation of a prisoner's daily life and specific tasks may prevent an individual from taking advantage of otherwise available services facilitating the exercise of religious freedom. As the decision itself demonstrates, prison authorities exercise ample discretion in such cases and their decisions are not subjected to most searching judicial scrutiny. Furthermore, believers who profess a creed which is

---

342. 61/1994 (IV. 20.) Korm. decree, Article 2.2. The phrase "historic churches" is on quote from the preamble of the decree.
343. 970/B/1994. AB decision, of 20 February 1995.
344. 13/2000 (VII. 14.) IM decree.
345. 30/1997 (X. 11.) NM decree. The decree provides that minors may exercise their religion within the house rules of the institution. The institution shall not keep any record of the minors' religious beliefs and shall not provide information to others (Article 24.1).

not included in the ordinary chaplaincy or pastoral scheme of a prison might face further difficulties, unless prison authorities are willing to undertake individual measures of accommodation. An example is known in the case *of X. v. the United Kingdom*[346] where prison authorities first made attempts to find a "Buddhist minister" for a Buddhist inmate, and – failing to do so – they allowed him extra correspondence with a fellow Buddhist.[347]

Regarding catering to religious needs in restricted environments, even the Krishnaswami study admits that in prisons it may not be possible to prepare food which conforms with religious dietary requirements. Nonetheless, in this respect, European democracies should also be mindful of Recommendation No. R (87) 3 of the Committee of Ministers to member states on prison rules[348] which also provides in rule 25.1 that "so far as possible" prisoners should be provided with food which conforms to the requirements of their religion.[349]

Limitations of religious freedom in prisons and the military

Due to the restricted nature of the military and prison environments, and the difficulties and shortcomings of accommodation, inmates and military personnel are often bound to experience such limitations of their rights and liberties which would be impermissible in normal circumstances. What makes these cases particularly interesting from a human rights perspective is the willingness of courts to accept justifications which do not live up to principles of constitutionalism outside these contexts.

The underlying principle of reviewing rights limitations in the armed forces was expressed by the ECtHR in *Engel v. The Netherlands*, where the justices said (para 57) that "a system of military discipline that by its very nature implied the possibility of placing on

---

346. *X. v. United Kingdom*, Application No. 5442/72 (1975) 1 D&R 41 260.
347. Petitioner challenged prison authorities' unwillingness to allow him to send an article to a Buddhist journal, thus preventing him from communicating with fellow Buddhists. The Commission declared the complaint inadmissible.
348. Adopted by the Committee of Ministers on 12 February 1987 at the 404th meeting of the Ministers' Deputies.
349. For an example, see Germany as described in Robbers, *Religious Freedom in Germany*, 2005, pp. 875-876.

certain of the rights and freedoms of the members of these forces limitations incapable of being imposed on civilians."[350] The Polish Constitutional Tribunal elaborated on the same concept in the following terms in a case which concerned the religious freedom of professional soldiers:

> Military service in every case is inherently connected with specified restrictions of an individual's freedom. Those restrictions sometimes touch on fundamental elements shaping the right to deciding on one's private life. At the same time, however, if they do not exceed the limits, resulting from nature of military service, of necessary (essential) rigours, which commonly, in every system accompany performing the function of a professional soldier or a soldier of professional service, the objection of infringement of the individual's fundamental rights could not be justified. There should be no doubts that the individual's rights collide in that case with purposefulness of protection of public interest, closely connected with protection of the State's security, so with that value, which in every democratic legal order can, within the limits indicated by essentiality, justify interference with the individual's rights, even with fundamental rights.[351]

The European Commission has not been welcoming about petitions challenging prison rules or practices which disallowed departures from prison uniform for reasons of conscience or religion. The compulsory wearing of prison clothes was found justified for reasons of prevention of disorder,[352] while the mandatory shaving of a Buddhist prisoner was regarded as a legitimate interference with freedom of religion and was found necessary for the protection of public order.[353] Paul Taylor argues that the prohibition of religious

---

350. *Engel v. The Netherlands* (No 1) (1976) 1 EHRR 647. Engel was not a case about religious freedom.
351. POL-1999-1-003 a) Poland / b) Constitutional Tribunal / c) / d) 16-02-1999 / e) SK 11/98 / f) / g) *Dziennik Ustaw Rzeczypospolitej Polskiej* (Official Gazette), 10.03.1999, item 182; *Orzecznictwo Trybunalu Konstytucyjnego Zbiór Urzedowy* (Official Digest), 1998, No. 2 / h) Codices (English, Polish). The case concerned the right of professional soldiers to terminate their contract for reasons of conscientious objection to military service.
352. *X. v. the United Kingdom*, Application No. 8231/78, DR 28 (1982) 5.
353. *X. v. Austria*, Application No. 1753/63, Yearbook VIII (1965) 174, 184.

clothing and wearing of religious symbols (including beards) shall not be treated as a manifestation of religious freedom, but as instance of coercion in a matter which falls within the *forum internum*.[354] Furthermore, Taylor points out that, in its jurisprudence, the UN Human Rights Committee is less forgiving about the limitation of prisoners' religious freedom. In *Boodoo v. Trinidad and Tobago*, the Human Rights Committee found that the forcible removal of the beard of a Muslim prisoner amounts to a violation of religious freedom (Article 18).[355]

Lack of access to objects required for religious exercise could give rise to further court cases. In the decision excerpted above, the Austrian Constitutional Court appears particularly considerate of a prisoner's request. Note, however, that courts are not always so considerate. When the Latvian Constitutional Court reviewed rules on solitary confinement it faced petitioners claiming that "confinement in a punishment cell or solitary confinement cell can be considered as cruel, inhuman and degrading treatment and should be qualified as torture, because: ... The challenged norms also prohibit the prisoner to take textbooks and religious literature to the solitary confinement or punishment cell as well as do not allow meeting the chaplain. Thus, the imprisoned have to backslide from their religious conviction and freedom of conscience." In its analysis, the Constitutional Court refused to address this objection altogether, thus remaining silent on the religious freedom issue.[356]

Indeed, it is a recurrent phenomenon in the above cases that courts are ready to accept justifications invoking the public interest, public order and military or prison discipline. The willingness of courts to be less protective of prisoners' religious freedom is explained in part by the fear that prisoners might abuse this opportunity.[357] In contrast, a factor which courts were ready to analyse in considerable

---

354. See Taylor, *Freedom of Religion*, p. 134.
355. *Boodoo v. Trinidad and Tobago*, Communication No. 721/1996, U.N. Doc. CCPR/C/74/D/721/1996 (2002).
356. Latvian Constitutional Court (LAT-2002-3-008 a) Latvia / b) Constitutional Court / c) / d) 22-10-2002 / e) 2002-04-03 / f) On the Compliance of Items 59.1.6, 66 and 68 of the "Rules on the Internal Order of Investigation Prisons" with Articles 89, 95 and 111 of the Constitution (Satversme) / g) *Latvijas Vestnesis* (Official Gazette), 154, 24.10.2002 / h) Codices (English, Latvian).)
357. Evans, C., *Freedom of Religion*, pp. 58-59.

detail in such cases was the contents and intensity of religious requirements prisoners were claiming to follow. In this respect it is sufficient to point to the decision of the Swiss Federal Court comparing the intensity of the requirement of Muslim believers' Friday prayers and the expectations attached to attendance at an Orthodox service. The European Commission is also known to have engaged in such an exercise in a case where it was ready to say that access to a Protestant pastor in a prison was just as good as if the prisoner could talk to an Anglican minister (as he himself wished).[358] The willingness of courts to engage in such an exercise is at least problematic as it suggests lower respect for the *forum internum* than witnessed in other cases.

Lastly, it is worth noting that so far the ECtHR did not find it necessary to depart from the basic premises of the Engel decision. Moreover, in *Kalaç v. Turkey*, when Turkish military officers complained about their forced retirement being brought via a disciplinary procedure allegedly owing to their Muslim belief, the ECtHR said that "in choosing to pursue a military career Mr Kalaç was accepting of his own accord a system of military discipline that by its very nature implied the possibility of placing on certain of the rights and freedoms of members of the armed forces limitations incapable of being imposed on civilians. States may adopt for their armies disciplinary regulations forbidding this or that type of conduct, in particular an attitude inimical to an established order reflecting the requirements of military service."[359] The ECtHR further observed that since disciplinary decision "was not based on Group Captain Kalaç's religious opinions and beliefs or the way he had performed his religious duties but on his conduct and attitude," there was no violation of religious freedom (Article 9) in the case.[360] Since then, Kalaç has been used to declare inadmissible a number of similar complaints.[361] One may regard this tendency as

---

358. *X. v. Germany*, Application No. 2413/65 (1966), 23 DR 1.
359. *Kalaç v. Turkey*, Application No. 20704/92, judgment of 1 July 1997, paragraph 28.
360. *Kalaç v. Turkey*, paragraph 30.
361. Martínez-Torrón, J., "Limitations on Religious Freedom in the Case Law of the European Court of Human Rights", 19, *Emory International Law Review*, 587, 2005, p. 602.

unfortunate in the light of reports that in Turkey, Muslim military officers face problems in their military career due to their religion.

Prohibition of taking advantage of a restricted environment

The cases above concerned the necessary extent of accommodation and limitations on religious freedom in restricted environments. A special problem arising in the prison and military problem stems from attempts to teach or promote one's religious or secular beliefs.

The German Constitutional Court warned in an early decision about potential dangers, putting the protection of human dignity in the centre of constitutional protection against attempts advocating conversion in a restricted environment. The German Constitutional Court emphasised the duty of the state to prevent the misuse of religious liberty. Thereafter, the Court said that:

> recruiting for a belief and convincing someone to turn from another belief, normally legal activities, become misuses of the basic right if the person tries, directly or indirectly, to use a base or immoral instrument to lure other persons from their beliefs. A person who exploits the special circumstances of penal servitude and promises and rewards someone with luxury goods in order to make him renounce his beliefs does not enjoy the benefit of protection under Article 4 of the Basic Law.[362]

Some strains of this judicial stance are traceable in a more recent decision in *Larissis v. Greece* where the ECtHR found that while proselytism within the army ranks imposed improper pressure on subordinates and therefore could be restricted under the Convention, yet proselytism by army officers *vis-à-vis* civilians was permissible and as such could not be limited. The ECtHR accepted that the hierarchical structures which are a feature of life in the armed forces may colour every aspect of the relations between military personnel, making it difficult for a subordinate to rebuff the approaches of an individual of superior rank or to withdraw from a conversation

---

362. *Tobacco Atheist case* (BvR 59/56). On quote in English in Kommers, *Constitutional Jurisprudence*, pp. 452-453.

initiated by him.[363] Thus, what would in the civilian world be seen as an innocuous exchange of ideas which the recipient is free to accept or reject, may, within the confines of military life, be viewed as a form of harassment or the application of undue pressure in abuse of power. It must be emphasised that not every discussion about religion or other sensitive matters between individuals of unequal rank will fall within this category. Nonetheless, where the circumstances so require, states may be justified in taking special measures to protect the rights and freedoms of subordinate members of the armed forces.

---

363. *Larissis v. Greece*, paragraph 51.

Chapter 4
Contemporary problems and challenges

The last chapter aims to contextualise some of the most controversial recent problems associated with the protection of religious freedom which affected various multi-religious polities in Europe. The first section centres on the prohibition of blasphemy, and on tensions the enforcement of blasphemy provisions might trigger.[364] The last section reflects on the emerging governmental obligation to protect polities against allegedly harmful sects and religious movements. As even this short overview of the present chapter suggests, most contemporary problems and challenges concerning religious freedom seem to involve participation of believers and their communities in the public space and in certain decisions on public affairs. An intensifying tension between the majority or dominant religion on the one hand, and new or minority religions on the other hand, is a recurring trait in all these contexts. The dilemmas and difficulties underlying the headscarf cases cast a long shadow over issues and problems addressed in the present chapter. As it will be demonstrated, preference given to or acquired by the culturally imbedded/historic/majority/prevailing religions, their organisations and believers prompts inequalities in the polity and sometimes unexpectedly escalates into such violations of religious freedom (and, ultimately, of personal autonomy and human dignity) which are incompatible with the requirements of

---

364. The section covers blasphemy regulations in a narrow sense (including the criminal prohibition of group defamation) and does not discuss incitement to religious or racial hatred.

state neutrality and secularity in a modern multicultural and multi-religious democracy.

4.1. The prohibition of blasphemy: Between freedom of expression and religious freedom

The criminal prohibition of blasphemy was preserved in the statute books of numerous European democracies almost without being invoked for much of the twentieth century. Blasphemy laws have recently come to attract attention in connection with expressions which were critical of Islam. The case which has attracted scholarly discussion since 1989 (without its forecasting potential having ever been truly exhausted) centres around a literary work believed by many Muslims to be disrespectful of Islam – the novel *Satanic Verses* by Salman Rushdie. The limits of freedom of expression in the name of respect for religious freedom were tested more recently on account of a set of cartoons on the Prophet Mohammed, which were originally published in the Danish newspaper *Jyllands-Posten* in the autumn of 2005.

It is a central premise of the following discussion that religious statements and perspectives form a part of the public discourse space and they are just as legitimate as any other expression which is critical of the tenets or teachings of a religion, its institutions or believers. Underlying the free speech jurisprudence of the European Court of Human Rights (ECtHR) is the principle expressed in *Handyside v. the United Kingdom* in the following terms:

> Freedom of expression constitutes one of the essential foundations of such a society, one of the basic conditions for its progress and for the development of every man. Subject to paragraph 2 of Article 10, it is applicable not only to "information" or "ideas" that are favourably received or regarded as inoffensive or as a matter of indifference, but also to those that offend, shock or disturb the State or any sector of the population. Such are the demands of that pluralism, tolerance and broadmindedness without which there is no "democratic society".[365]

---

365. *Handyside v. the United Kingdom*, Application No. 5493/72, judgment of 7 December 1976, paragraph 49.

Legal regulations prohibiting blasphemy constitute an exception to this principle on the permissible scope and limitations of freedom of expression – an exception which brings with it a wide range of problems. To begin with, the mainstream interpretation of blasphemy provisions tends to have a Christian orientation even in European countries where such criminal prohibitions do not appear on their face to protect the basic tenets of a particular established or majority religion. Thus, blasphemy clauses offer a clear opportunity for discrimination upon beliefs. In practice, this results in a public discourse where unprivileged creeds have to withstand claims which cannot be made about protected religions and their believers.

Furthermore, the prohibition of blasphemy provisions imposes a clear limitation on freedom of expression in the name of protecting religious values, sentiments or the religious freedom of others, and as such presents an opportunity for an open clash between two fundamental rights. Attempts at resolving such a conflict are at the heart of jurisprudence on blasphemy. The difficulty lies in the fact that while freedom of speech or artistic freedom is not absolute, the protection of religious sensitivities does not appear to be a sound reason justifying limitations imposed upon free speech, nor does the protection of freedom of religion entail a right to have one's religious beliefs respected by others either. Respect for freedom of religion does not "not necessarily and in all circumstances imply a right to bring any specific form of proceedings against those who ... offend the sensitivities of an individual or of a group of individuals."[366] The protection of religious freedom may require governments to enact legislation which protects believers from interference with their religious exercise, for instance from disturbing their religious worship, but does not secure protection against insult or criticism of one's their religious beliefs.[367] Failing to acknowledge such basic premises of rights protection may have devastating consequences not only for the public discourse, but

---

366. See *Choudhury v. the United Kingdom*, Application No. 17439/90 (1991) (the decision where the Commission found the complaint submitted against the United Kingdom for failing to prosecute Salman Rushdie for blasphemy on account of his *Satanic Verses* inadmissible), as summarised in another admissibility decision: *Dubowska & Skup v. Poland*, Application No. 33490/96, Decision of 18 April 1997 (inadmissible).

367. Also in *Dubowska & Skup v. Poland*.

also for the enjoyment of basic human rights and the preservation of public peace.

> ### Case law
>
> - ITA-2001-1-001 a) Italy / b) Constitutional Court / c) / d) 13-11-2000 / e) 508/2000 / f) / g) *Gazzetta Ufficiale, Prima Serie Speciale* (Official Gazette), 49/29.11.2000 / h) Codices (Italian).
>
> The Constitutional Court declares unconstitutional, on the grounds of infringement of Article 3 of the Constitution (which sets out the principle of equality of all citizens without distinction as to religion) and Article 8 of the Constitution (which establishes the equal freedom of all religious denominations before the law), the article of the Penal Code which lays down a prison sentence of up to one year for "anyone publicly insulting the state religion", that is, the Catholic religion.
>
> The impugned provision, which was enacted in 1930, and all the others that establish special protection for the state (Catholic) religion are explained by the fact that political circles at the time considered Catholicism as a factor of the national's moral unity. The Catholic religion was the "only" state religion (according to the wording of Article 1 of the Albertino Statute, subsequently incorporated into the 1929 concordat between the Holy See and Italy), and was therefore specially protected, even within the framework of state interests.
>
> This legislative approach was subsequently abandoned. On the one hand, the additional protocol to the agreement amending the Lateran Pact specified that the Catholic religion was no longer the sole state religion, and on the other, in the context of agreements concluded with non-Catholic denominations as laid down in Article 8 of the Constitution, equal penal protection was ensured (agreement with the Union of Italian Jewish Communities), or else direct penal protection was renounced (agreements with the Waldenses, the Assemblies of God in Italy and the Italian Baptist Evangelical Christian Union).

Therefore, the article of the criminal code providing for a prison sentence of up to one year for "anyone publicly insulting the state religion" is an anachronism which, in view of the legislator's inertia, must be eliminated by the Constitutional Court. In the criminal law field, equality can only be restored by eliminating the offence formerly created, because the Court has rejected any "additive" approach extending protection under criminal law to other hitherto excluded religions.

Commentary

Blasphemy is an elusive concept, withstanding attempts at precise definition. The Irish Constitution expressly authorises the prohibition of speech on or publication of blasphemous or seditious material (Article 40.6.1.i). Nonetheless, when the Supreme Court of Ireland was to apply the common law of blasphemous libel, the Irish justices refused to do so, as – lacking a statutory definition of blasphemy – they claimed not to have found sufficient guidance in the common law to proceed.[368]

In general terms, the prohibition of blasphemy is directed against any expression of disrespect, hostility or irreverence towards or contempt of God or the sacred, or religious institutions, ceremonies or officials.[369] Thus, on their face, laws prohibiting blasphemy impose a limitation on freedom of expression and artistic freedom in order to protect God and religion from false claims and insults. Consider

---

368. *Corway v. Independent Newspapers (Ireland) Limited* [1999] IESC 5; [1999] 4 IR 485; [2000] 1 ILRM 426 (30 July 1999), paragraph 38 ("In this state of the law, and in the absence of any legislative definition of the constitutional offence of blasphemy, it is impossible to say of what the offence of blasphemy consists. As the Law Reform Commission has pointed out neither the *actus reus* nor the *mens rea* is clear. The task of defining the crime is one for the Legislature, not for the Courts. In the absence of legislation and in the present uncertain state of the law the Court could not see its way to authorising the institution of a criminal prosecution for blasphemy against the Respondents.")

369. For comprehensive criminal protection of religious freedom, religious officials, ceremonies and believers via means other than the offence of blasphemy, see Belgian Criminal Code, Articles 142-146. Described in Torfs, R., "The Permissible Scope of Legal Limitations on the Freedom of Religion or Belief in Belgium", 19, *Emory International Law Review*, 637, 2005, pp. 654-655.

the Austrian blasphemy provision which was at the centre of attention in the ECtHR's *Otto Preminger v. Austria* which reads as:

> Whoever, in circumstances where his behaviour is likely to arouse justified indignation, disparages or insults a person who, or an object which, is an object of veneration of a church or religious community established within the country, or a dogma, a lawful custom or a lawful institution of such a church or religious community, shall be liable to a prison sentence of up to six months or a fine of up to 360 daily rates.[370]

Although the clash between freedom of expression and religious freedom is apparent, several European democracies retain a prohibition of blasphemy.[371] While most European constitutions and international instruments lack such express provisions, blasphemy (or a functional equivalent) stands as a separate crime in several national criminal codes in Europe. These provisions differ in their scope and intensity of prohibition. As a general trend, blasphemy provisions are relatively rarely invoked in Europe and their enforcement is not prevalent. Nonetheless, the ECtHR remains to be of the view that the prohibition of blasphemy does not violate the Convention *per se*, as there is no consensus among the member states for its abolition.[372]

In his oft-quoted article, when exploring the origins of the English common law crime of blasphemy, Robert Post explains that "blasphemy in its early years was more closely allied with sedition (than with obscenity), since attacks on God and religion were viewed as attacks on the social order."[373] Blasphemy as a crime started

---

370. Austrian Penal Code, Section 188, on quote in *Otto Preminger Institut v. Austria*, Application No. 13470/87, judgment of 20 September 1994, paragraph 25.
371. On blasphemy from a free speech perspective, see Barendt, E., *Freedom of Speech*, second edition, 2005, pp. 186 et seq.
372. See *I. A. v. Turkey*, Application No. 42571/98, judgment of 13 September 2005, paragraph 25 and in *Aydin Tatlav v. Turkey*, Application No. 50692/99, judgment of 2 May 2006, paragraph 24, both quoting *Otto Preminger Institut v. Austria*, Application No. 13470/87, judgment of 20 September 1994, paragraph 49, also in *Wingrove v. the United Kingdom*, Application No. 17419/90, judgment of 25 November 1996, paragraph 57.
373. Post, R., "Cultural Heterogeneity and the Law: Pornography, Blasphemy, and the First Amendment", 76, *California Law Review*, 297, 1988, p. 306.

to transform in *Regina v. Hetherington*,[374] where Lord Denning's charge to the jury put the emphasis not on the substance of what was said, but on the manner of the expression. While he viewed a discussion tolerable which was "carried on in a sober and temperate and decent style" (even if its contents were problematic from a criminal law perspective), "insult and ridicule, which leaves the judgment really not free to act" was to be prohibited. The same line of thought was followed later by Lord Coleridge when he said that in order to be blasphemous, expression must be "calculated and insult the feelings and the deepest religious convictions of the great majority of persons amongst whom we live. ... If the decencies of controversy are observed, even the fundamentals of religion may be attacked without the writer being guilty of blasphemy."[375] A similar aim is apparent in the Polish Criminal Code where the blasphemy provision focuses not on the protection of the religious doctrines or deities, but on the feelings of believers and the integrity of places of worship.[376]

Thus, it is apparent from Post's findings that blasphemy provisions are best understood as instruments aimed at protecting public peace via preventing utterances which might offend the religious sentiments of a group of believers, who typically constitute the majority. This is in line with the views of Lord Scarman on the rationale behind the common law offence of blasphemous libel, as stated in *Whitehouse v. Lemon*:

> The offence belongs to a group of criminal offences designed to safeguard the internal tranquillity of the kingdom. In an increasingly plural society such as that of modern Britain it is necessary not only to respect the differing religious beliefs, feelings and practices of all but also to protect them from scurrility, vilification, ridicule and contempt... I will not lend my voice to a view of the law relating to blasphemous libel

---

374. *Regina v. Hetherington*, 4 St. Tr. N.S. 593 (1841).
375. Lord Coleridge on quote in Post, *Cultural Heterogeneity*, p. 308.
376. Quoted from *Dubowska & Skup v. Poland*.

which would render it a dead letter, or diminish its efficacy to protect religious feelings from outrage and insult.[377]

While the protection of public peace (or prevention of a breach of the peace) might be an honest motivation behind blasphemy laws, it is important to point out at the outset that blasphemy rules are not to be confused with legal regulation prohibiting hate speech or hate crimes targeting particular religious groups or institutions. As a proper example of an act prohibiting religious hatred, consider the recently enacted Racial and Religious Hatred Act 2006 of the United Kingdom. The act prohibits various forms of behaviour (including speech, publishing or broadcasting materials, etc.) which are intended to stir up religious hatred via threatening "a group of persons defined by reference to religious belief or lack of religious belief."[378]

Despite its firm stance expressed in *Handyside v. the United Kingdom* offering protection to shocking and offensive speech under Article 10, the ECtHR does not find national criminal laws prohibiting blasphemy *per se* in violation of freedom of expression. Nonetheless, the ECtHR was not at ease when determining what legitimate aim (if any) such regulations served. In *Otto Preminger Institut v. Austria*, the first major decision on blasphemy, the ECtHR said that the purpose of the Austrian criminal prohibition of blasphemy was "to protect the right of citizens not to be insulted in their religious feelings by the public expression of views of other persons."[379] Subsequently, in *Murphy v. Ireland*, the ECtHR added that:

> a wider margin of appreciation is generally available to the Contracting States when regulating freedom of expression in relation to matters liable to offend intimate personal convictions within the sphere of morals or, especially, religion. Moreover, as in the field of morals, and perhaps to an even

---

377. *Whitehouse v. Lemon* [1979] 1 All ER 898, pp. 921-922. Note that Lord Scarman said in the case that blasphemy protection shall be extended to non-Christians.
378. The terminology used above repeats verbatim the language of the central provisions of the act. Note that the act clearly distinguishes racial hatred from religious hatred.
379. *Otto Preminger Institut v. Austria*, paragraph 48. See also *Wingrove v. United Kingdom*, paragraph 47.

greater degree, there is no uniform European conception of the requirements of "the protection of the rights of others" in relation to attacks on their religious convictions. What is likely to cause substantial offence to persons of a particular religious persuasion will vary significantly from time to time and from place to place, especially in an era characterised by an ever growing array of faiths and denominations.[380]

The *prima facie* difference between Post's findings concerning the aim of blasphemy laws and the ECtHR's is less a matter of grand theory than sheer practicality. Under the European Convention, the search for an acceptable justification is framed by the language of Article 10.2 which allows for such grounds as "the interests of national security, territorial integrity or public safety, for the prevention of disorder or crime, for the protection of health or morals, for the protection of the reputation or the rights of others, for preventing the disclosure of information received in confidence, or for maintaining the authority and impartiality of the judiciary." Thus, the ECtHR had to fit whatever justification it found underlying blasphemy laws in one of these categories, of which the "protection of the rights of others" seemed most convenient. As Eric Barendt notes, it is possible that there is a proper way to justify restrictions imposed upon blasphemous speech, but so far the ECtHR did not manage to reveal such a justification.[381]

In its recent jurisprudence on blasphemy laws – and departing from its free speech jurisprudence in cases without a religious thread – the ECtHR seems to emphasise the need for respect towards the feelings and sensitivities of believers. Unfortunately, however, the current approach leaves national courts and ultimately the ECtHR to concentrate on what is disrespectful of the religious feelings of particular groups of believers in a given case. A recent instance was *I.A. v. Turkey* where the judges disagreed on whether passages in a novel constituted such an "abusive attack on the Prophet of

---

380. *Murphy v. Ireland*, Application No. 44179/98, judgment of 10 July 2003, paragraph 67.
For a detailed analysis of the difference between the ECtHR's position on the issue of legitimate aim in *Otto Preminger Institut v. Austria* and *Murphy v. Ireland*, see Taylor, P. M., *Freedom of Religion, UN and European Human Rights Law and Practice*, Cambridge, 2005, pp. 88 et seq.
381. Barendt, *Freedom of Speech*, p. 192.

Islam" due to which "believers may legitimately feel themselves to be the object of unwarranted and offensive attacks"[382] – speech which was found unprotected under Article 10 of the Convention. Note, furthermore, that even if one accepts respect for the feelings and sensitivities of believers as a legitimate aim behind blasphemy laws, it remains largely unclear how silencing voices disrespectful of believers or their beliefs will contribute to protecting those believers' religious freedom.

Note that at times, blasphemy is not phrased as a specific criminal prohibition devoted to blasphemy, but is banned indirectly. The Slovakian Criminal Code, for instance, includes a provision on group defamation (Article 198.1.b), prohibiting the defamation in public of "a group of inhabitants of the republic for their political belief, faith or because they have no religion."[383] This clause was used to convict a journalist who wrote a piece criticising an archbishop in a weekly paper, among other things, for the monsignor's statement concerning the posters for the film, *The People vs. Larry Flynt*.[384] In *Klein v. Slovakia*, the ECtHR quashed the decisions of the domestic courts, finding that the article was directed at a particular person (that is, the archbishop) and not the entire faith as such, nor did it constitute an interference with the rights of believers.[385]

Furthermore, it is important to point out that provisions attaching negative legal consequences to blasphemous speech may be contained not only in criminal codes, but also in civil codes or regulation on the press and media.[386] The day-to-day application of such provisions is often left with lower domestic courts in cases where constitutional arguments are not necessarily addressed. Consider, for instance, a case involving a French paper, *Libération,* which ran a cartoon showing as its central figure a naked Jesus Christ wearing only a condom. His figure was surrounded by several bishops, one of whom was saying "He sure would have worn a condom!"

---

382. *I. A. v. Turkey*, paragraph 29.
383. English translation quoted from *Klein v. Slovakia*, Application No. 72208/01, judgment of 31 October 2006, paragraph 32.
384. The case reached the ECtHR as *Klein v. Slovakia*.
385. *Klein v. Slovakia*, paragraphs 51 and 52.
386. Note that *Wingrove v. the United Kingdom* was not a criminal case but one classification of a film for distribution, while *Murphy v. Ireland* a blasphemy prohibition in broadcasting law.

A Christian NGO (*Alliance Générale contre le Racisme et pour le Respect de l'Identité Française et Chrétienne*) sought action against the paper under the French press law[387] which – in its chapter on "Offences against persons" (*Délits contre les personnes*) – defines as insult, such outraging or contemptuous expressions which do not contain a statement of fact (Article 29.2), and prescribes an aggravated punishment for insults concerning a group of persons due to their religious beliefs (Article 33.3). Upholding the decision of lower courts, in 2006, the Paris court of appeal[388] found that the cartoon does not constitute insult against a religious group, as all the cartoon intended was to draw attention to the need for condoms in the fight against HIV/AIDS, especially in Africa.[389]

On the application of a media law provision protecting the feelings of believers, one has to look at Poland, where the 1992 Law on Radio and Television Broadcasting prohibits the infringement of the religious feelings of receivers and requires broadcasting organisations to respect Christian values corresponding with universal ethical rules. Emphasising that the rules should not become a basis for preliminary restraints, the Polish Constitutional Tribunal upheld these provisions saying the law does not discriminate against any religion. "The direction to respect 'Christian values' contained in the Law on Radio and Television Broadcasting, is given by way of example only, and is justified by the Christian tradition and culture of the Polish society, irrespective of an individual's personal feelings. In the Tribunal's opinion, a broadcast that is inconsistent with values other than Christian values may also be disrespectful of the religious feelings of the receivers, irrespective of each individual's religion" (Decision POL-1994-2-009 a) Poland / b) Constitutional Tribunal / c) / d) 07-06-1994 / e) K 17/93 / f) / g) *Orzecznictwo Trybunału Konstytucyjnego* (Official Digest), 1994, vol. 1, item 11 / h) Codices

---

387. La loi du 29 juillet 1881 sur la liberté de la presse. Note that in France blasphemy is not a criminal offence.
388. *Cour d'appel de Paris*, 11th chamber, per judge Laurence Trebucq.
389. Reported by AFP on 17 May 2006. On quote as "Le Christ affublé d'un préservatif: Libération gagne en appel contre l'Agrif", at: http://www.minorites.org/article.php?IDA=16412.

(Polish)).³⁹⁰ Note, however, that expression which is perceived as anti-Catholic appears to attract high fines, while comments which were understood as openly anti-Semitic did not trigger action by the Polish media board applying the law.³⁹¹

Irrespective of actual justifications underlying the enactment or retention of criminal prohibitions on blasphemy, it seems to be the case that where criminal blasphemy provisions are applied, their interpretation favours the (once) official, prevailing or majority religion. Thus, in most European democracies which retain this crime, the application of blasphemy provisions tends to favour Christian religions, irrespective of the wording of the actual clause. Speaking from a US experience, Christopher Eisgruber and Lawrence Sager submit that:

> the secular goal upon which religious liberty rests (is) the equality of persons. So, for example, the government cannot execute heretics, enforce blasphemy laws, condition access to office on one's religious affiliation, single out religious rituals for special burdens. ... If the government discriminates against particular believers in any of the ways just mentioned, it is behaving unjustly. ... That is the point of equal regard, and that is the point of religious liberty.³⁹²

As the development of Italian constitutional jurisprudence illustrates, Italian constitutional justices were sensitive to this problem. The Italian Constitutional Court reached its decision on the unconstitutionality of the criminal prohibition of "publicly insulting the state religion" gradually, upon challenges which submitted that the provision which protected the Catholic religion only

---

390. The long excerpts from the decision are available in English on the website of the Polish Constitutional Tribunal in English at: http://www.trybunal.gov.pl/eng/Judical_Decisions/1986_1999/K_%2017_93a.pdf.

391. For a report on a recent incident, see Richard Bernstein, "Letter from Poland, Differing Treatment of Religious Slurs Raise an Old Issue", *The New York Times*, 3 May 2006. Also available at: http://www.nytimes.com/2006/05/03/world/03letter.html?ex=1304308800&en=796ae59cc87cf0f6&ei=5088&partner=rssnyt&emc=rss.

392. Eisgruber, C., and Sager, L., "Unthinking Religious Freedom", 74, *Texas Law Review*, 1996, pp. 600-608.

was discriminatory.³⁹³ In 1973, the Constitutional Court rejected the petition altogether, while in 1988, the Court admitted that the official recognition of other religions started to undermine the rationale of the law. In 1995, the Constitutional Court then said that the Criminal Code's blasphemy provision was discriminatory. In this case, the Constitutional Court abolished the rule applicable to the symbols of the Catholic religion, while noting that it was beyond the powers of the Court to extend the provision to other religions (Decision ITA-1995-3-014 a) Italy / b) Constitutional Court / c) / d) 18-10-1995 / e) 440/1995 / f) / g) *Gazzetta Ufficiale, Prima Serie Speciale* (Official Gazette), 44, 25.10.1995 / h) Codices (Italian)). The Constitutional Court's decision of 2000 abolishing the blasphemy provision altogether fits in this line of jurisprudence.³⁹⁴

The Italian experience is in sharp contrast with Spanish constitutional developments. As Javier Martínez-Torrón explains, in Spain the criminal protection of religion:

> consists in penalizing blasphemy as well as public abuse or derision of a religion and its tenets or rites. During Spain's history as a confessional state, Spanish criminal law specifically protected Catholicism. In 1983, the Criminal Code was amended to extend its protection of the population's religious sentiments to all religious denominations … In 1984 … [Constitutional] Court affirmed that penalizing blasphemy "does not imply that a determined church or religious denomination is granted a privileged treatment, for the idea of God or the notion of the sacred are not the exclusive patrimony of any of them in particular." Similarly in 1986, the Court held that the crime of offence to religion – public abuse or derision – did not violate the constitutional principle of neutrality,

---

393. See Nardini, W. J., "Passive Activism and the Limits of Judicial Self-restraint: Lessons for America from the Italian Constitutional Court", 30, *Seton Hall Law Review*, 1, 1999, p. 10. The rule was contained in Article 402 of the Italian Criminal Code.

394. Note that the Italian Criminal Code retains several provisions protecting religious freedom. In particular, criminal protection covers believers and ministers of the Catholic churches and of other admitted religions (*un culto ammesso nello Stato*) (Articles 403 and 406), and places and ceremonies of Catholic worship and of other admitted religions (Articles 404 and 405, together with 406). Offences against admitted religions trigger lighter sentences (Article 406), thus preferential treatment for the Catholic Church is still preserved.

since Article 209 of the Criminal Code had been amended in 1983 to eliminate the reference to "the Catholic Church or other confessions legally recognized." Consequently, the protection offered by the Criminal Code covered every religion and not only a particular church ... Moreover, the Court declared that a religiously neutral state may use criminal laws to protect the population's religious sentiments because such state action pursues the legitimate aim of safeguarding its citizens' rights and freedoms, particularly their freedom of religion.[395]

The predominantly Christian orientation of blasphemy provisions and their application exhibits a high potential for discrimination against non-Christian religions, thus easily distorting the public discourse, as blasphemy rules thus interpreted protect criticism of non-Christian religions in a fashion which is not tolerated in the case of Christian religions.[396] This disparity produced a favourable unintended consequence in the case of Salman Rushdie against whom – following the fatwa issue by the Ayatollah Khomeini[397] – private prosecution was sought for blasphemous libel in England. English courts were of the opinion that Rushdie could not commit blasphemous libel as the common law of blasphemy can only be invoked against Christian religions.[398] (Note that irrespective of the outcome of the case commentators argue that it would have been

---

395. Martínez-Torrón, J., "Freedom of Religion in the Case Law of the Spanish Constitutional Court", 2001, *Brigham Young University Law Review*, 711, 2001, adding that "Spain's new Criminal Code, enacted in 1995, has continued the practice of criminalizing abuse or derision of religion, at the same time providing that the same punishment must be imposed for public offences against non-believers."
396. See, in particular, Loveland, I., *Constitutional Law, Administrative Law and Human Rights*, Oxford, 2004, third edition, p. 592.
397. The fatwa is reprinted in English in Arjomand, S. A., "Religious Human Rights and the Principle of Legal Pluralism in the Middle East", pp. 331-348, van der Vyver, J., and Witte, J., Jr., eds, *Religious Human Rights in Global Perspective: Legal Perspectives*, Martinus Nijhoff, 1996, p. 343. The fact that following a fatwa a bounty was offered by another cleric was so far unprecedented.
398. *Regina v. Chief Metropolitan Stipendiary Magistrate ex parte Choudhury* [1990] 3 WLR 986. The case was brought via private prosecution.

Contemporary problems and challenges

inappropriate for the courts to expand the scope of the common law rule to cover non-Christian religions.[399])

As this short account on blasphemy laws duly demonstrates, the prohibition of blasphemy does allow for inappropriate distinctions between faiths. In extreme cases, blasphemy laws may offer means to a willing government to suppress unpopular religious movements. Court decisions which treat blasphemy laws as legitimate restrictions on freedom of expression have the potential to undermine the basic tenets of free speech protection under the auspices of protecting the religious sensitivities (and not necessarily religious freedom) of certain segments of the polity. Blasphemy laws are problematic because their application often blurs the line between content-based restrictions and the prohibition of conveying a message in a particular manner (e.g. incitement). Further problems arise from the fact that very often allegedly blasphemous expressions take the form of caricatures, sarcastic pieces or works of art. Principles derived in such cases on the permissible scope of speech might be viewed as applicable not only in such instances but may have a radiating effect on non-artistic forms of expression, and also on expression.

When looking for potential justifications for limiting freedom of expression via blasphemy laws, the ultimate question is whether failing to prohibit blasphemous expressions prevents anyone from exercising their freedom of religion. Lacking such an effect or impact, blasphemy provisions constitute a burden of freedom of expression which is not acceptable in a constitutional democracy benefiting from a robust public discourse. An approach which properly respects freedom of expression will concentrate on curbing hateful utterances threatening believers, but would leave unrestricted the simply hurtful, the insulting and the offensive.

Before concluding this section, note shall be made of the Danish cartoon controversy. Caricatures depicting the Prophet Mohammed made a career in international human rights circles not so much due to concerns about the proper scope of blasphemy laws in Europe, but because their publication triggered a wave of deadly

---

399. See, for example, James, J. and Ghandi, S., "The English Law of Blasphemy and the European Convention on Human Rights", 1998, *European Human Rights Law Review*, 430, 1998, pp. 448 et seq.

violence, diplomatic complications and a boycott of Danish goods around the globe.[400] On account of the Danish cartoons, several Muslim leaders urged blasphemy prosecutions against national newspapers which ran the cartoons. After criminal prosecution for blasphemy was dropped, a Danish court also threw out a civil libel claim against the paper which first published the cartoons.[401] At the same time, persons involved in organising violent protests against Danish embassies abroad were convicted[402] along with newspaper editors who agreed to reprint the cartoons in Islamic countries.[403]

Following this wave of violence, discussion on legitimate criticism of religious teachings and their followers got regrettably tangled in a web of calls for expanding the scope of blasphemy legislation, arguments for strengthening hate speech and hate crime legislation (which often failed to distinguish racial from religious hate), and discussions on a series of other measures limiting the exercise of human rights which capitalise on a fear of Islam across the European continent. National governments were urged or tempted to pass legislation curbing speech which was disrespectful

---

400. It is not possible to analyse here, to what extent had this deadly wave been used for local political benefits in Islamic countries.
401. "Danish Court reject Cartoon Suit", *BBC News*, Thursday, 26 October 2006, at: http://news.bbc.co.uk/2/hi/europe/6087506.stm. Petitioners, several Muslim organisations, argued that the caricatures "attacked the honour of believers because they portrayed the Prophet as war-like and criminal and made a clear link between Muhammad, war and terrorism." The Danish court did not find the cartoons offensive.
402. For example, "Cartoons Protester Faces Retrial", *BBC News*, Monday, 13 November 2006, at: http://news.bbc.co.uk/2/hi/uk_news/6143340.stm. In the United Kingom, Mizanur Rahman was found guilty of incitement to racial hatred, but the jury was divided on the charge of incitement to murder, and therefore the crown is seeking a retrial in his case.
403. See "Second Yemeni editor convicted", *BBC News*, Wednesday, 6 December 2006, at: http://news.bbc.co.uk/2/hi/middle_east/6213032.stm. Both Yemeni editors were convicted for denigrating Islam. They defended their decision to reprint the Danish cartoons as an attempt to show how insulting the drawings were.

of religions or their believers, and also to pass rules prohibiting religious hate speech.[404]

A clash of fundamental rights is never simple to resolve. The case of the Danish cartoons demonstrates the difficulty with placing the issue and its implications on the right scale. Flemming Rose, the culture editor of the *Jyllands Posten*, revealed the reasons behind the publication of the cartoons in the following terms:

> I commissioned the cartoons in response to several incidents of self-censorship in Europe caused by widening fears and feelings of intimidation in dealing with issues related to Islam ... The cartoonists treated Islam the same way they treat Christianity, Buddhism, Hinduism and other religions. And by treating Muslims in Denmark as equals they made a point: We are integrating you into the Danish tradition of satire because you are part of our society, not strangers. The cartoons are including, rather than excluding, Muslims.[405]

In order to assess editor Rose's argument, it is worth taking into account that according to recent statistics, the Muslim community is the second largest in Denmark (with approximately 210 000 believers, amounting to 3.7% of the population), in a country where 83% of the population belongs with the official Evangelical Lutheran Church.[406] Yet, as an editorial in the *New York Times* – one of the many major papers which refused to reprint the cartoons – pointed out, the cartoons were largely unnoticed outside Denmark "until a group of Muslim leaders there made a point of circulating them, along with drawings far more offensive than the relatively mild stuff actually printed by the paper, *Jyllands-Posten*. It's far from the first time that an almost-forgotten incident has been

---

404. Note that similar claims were made in the Netherlands following the murder of film director, Theo Van Gogh, who likened Muslims to "goat fuckers" and "pimps of the Prophet". See "Dutch blasphemy law faces the chop", of 16 November 2004, available at: http://www.expatica.com/actual/article.asp?subchannel_id=1&story_id=13966.

405. Rose, F., "Why I Published Those Cartoons", *The Washington Post*, Sunday, 19 February 2006; Page B01, available at: http://www.washingtonpost.com/wp-dyn/content/article/2006/02/17/AR2006021702499.html.

406. Source: *Denmark, International Religious Freedom Report 2006*, available at: http://www.state.gov/g/drl/rls/irf/2006/71377.htm. Third in line are Catholics, a group of approximately 35 000.

dredged up to score points with the public during politically sensitive times."[407] What the Danish editors did not consider was the global conundrum triggered by the cartoons. Note, however, that the global perspective focuses on the clash of civilisations and the need to reduce such tension not so much for the sake of protecting free speech or religious freedom, but primarily in order to reduce international security risks and consolidate corporate earnings in global markets.

4.2. On the governmental obligation to protect against dangerous religions

As was mentioned in Chapter 1, in European constitutional scholarship and jurisprudence, the view that the government shall take positive measures in order to foster the enjoyment of constitutional rights is persistent. In the sphere of religious freedoms, the government's positive obligation to promote the enjoyment of rights associated with free exercise takes either the form of claims for accommodation or appear in discussions of church–state relations. Nonetheless, when discussing potential limitations on religious freedom, it is important to be mindful of a relatively recent development premised on an understanding of governments as protectors of the well-being of the polity.

> *Case law*
>
> ■ GER-2002-H-001 a) Germany / b) Federal Constitutional Court / c) First Panel / d) 26-06-2002 / e) 1 BvR 670/91 / f) / g) *Entscheidungen des Bundesverfassungsgerichts* (Official Digest), 105, pp. 279-312 / h) *Neue Juristische Wochenschrift*, 2002, pp. 2626-2632; *Europäische Grundrechte Zeitschrift*.
>
> Since the 1960s, previously unknown groups have manifested themselves in the Federal Republic of Germany. They

---

407. Editorial, "Those Danish Cartoons", *The New York Times*, 7 February 2006, available at: http://www.nytimes.com/2006/02/07/opinion/07tue2.html?ex=1296968400&en=1ab8b066d9b6fc27&ei=5090&partner=rssuserland&emc=rss. See Arjomand arguing that in the Muslim world the Rushdie affair was more a political case, than a legal, at Arjomand, "Religious Human Rights in the Middle East", p. 343.

immediately attracted public interest and have been described as "sects", "youth sects", "youth religions", "psycho sects", "psycho groups" or similar names. The groups have quickly become the subject of critical public debate due to the fact that they understand their goals to be predominantly influenced by their religious and philosophical views and due to their methods of treating members and followers. Such groups were accused, in particular, of isolating their members from the outside world, alienating them especially from their own families, manipulating them psychologically and exploiting them financially.

Since the 1970s, this phenomenon and the movements behind the groups have also occupied the federal and *Länder* (state) governments. On many occasions, governmental statements have been issued on the problems associated with these groups in reply to parliamentary questions. The federal and *Länder* governments have also informed the public about such groups directly in brochures, press releases and speeches. As part of their public relations work, state agencies have characterised the movement involved in this case as a "sect," "youth sect," "youth religion" and "psycho sect". The attributes "destructive" and "pseudo-religious" have also been used against it, and the accusation has been raised that its members have been manipulated.

...

Members of [meditation societies of what is known as the Shree Rajneesh, Bhagwan or Osho movement] have demanded in several original proceedings before the administrative courts that the Federal Republic of Germany desist from issuing statements about the religious movement and the societies belonging to it. The feeling was that such statements were incriminating. After the complainants had been unsuccessful in all instances, they lodged a constitutional complaint and essentially alleged that their freedom to profess a religious or philosophical creed under Article 4.1 of the Basic Law had been infringed.

... The government's duty to provide direction for the state includes assisting members of the public in coping with conflicts within the state and society by providing them with information on a timely basis. The government must also face challenges even if they occur at short notice, react quickly and properly to crises and the worries of citizens and help citizens to find their bearings.

...

The federal government is bound by the standards inherent in the proportionality principle when it provides information. Statements which impair the scope of protection contained in Articles 4.1 and 4.2 of the Basic Law must be appropriate, in particular, in relation to the event which provoked them.

According to these standards, the characterisation of the philosophical groups which are the subject of the proceedings as "sect", "youth religion", "youth sect" and "psycho sect" is not from the point of view of constitutional law open to objection. The employment of these terms satisfies the requirement that the state be neutral in religious or philosophical matters. It does not affect the scope of protection under Articles 4.1 and 4.2 of the Basic Law.

On the other hand, labels such as "destructive" and "pseudo-religious" and an accusation of manipulation do not satisfy the requirements of constitutional law.

Even if the employment of such terms could not be criticised on the grounds that it exceeded the powers of the federal government, nonetheless the terms used infringed the neutrality requirement and were thus not justifiable according to the proportionality principle. In particular, no substantiated reasons were advanced, which could justify the statements regarded as defamatory by the complainants, nor were any such reasons otherwise apparent. They also do not arise from the situation in which the assessments by the federal government were made.

- BEL-2000-1-003 a) Belgium / b) Court of Arbitration / c) / d) 21-03-2000 / e) 31/2000 / f) / g) *Moniteur belge* (Official Gazette), 22.04.2000 / h) Codices (French, German, Dutch).

An anthroposophical movement (the "Steiner" movement) applied to the Court to set aside the Act of 2 June 1998 setting up a centre to provide information and advice on harmful sectarian organisations and an administrative unit to co-ordinate efforts to combat harmful sectarian organisations.

> The act's aim is to monitor the phenomenon of sects and their practices. It applies to "harmful sectarian organisations", in other words "any group with a philosophical or religious function, whether real or supposed, which, in its organisation or practices, engages in unlawful, harmful activities, causes harm to individuals or society or infringes human dignity".
>
> ... The Court found that the act sought to give effect to a recommendation by a parliamentary commission of inquiry and a recommendation by the Council of Europe Parliamentary Assembly.
>
> The Court did not uphold the applicant's claim that the contested act would introduce discriminatory, preventive supervision, whereas penalties for illegal activities could only be issued retroactively and only groups with a philosophical or religious function would be affected. The act did not actually give the new centre any powers regarding advance monitoring and prevention of the expression of opinions and did not require authorisation before an association of any kind was formed. With regard to the restriction of the act to harmful groups with a philosophical or religious function, the Court noted: "It is precisely the philosophical or religious nature, whether real or supposed, of these organisations which appears to make them attractive to a proportion of the population. This explains the particular concern which the act in question sets out to address." The safeguards laid down in the act itself mean that there is no additional interference with the protection of privacy: personal data can only be processed by the centre in connection with tasks prescribed by law.

Commentary

New religious movements and the label of brainwashing

The appearance of new religious movements which attract believers seems to almost automatically trigger speculations. In addition to the terms "sect" and "cult", the fuzzy concept of brainwashing appears frequently in these dicussions. Brainwashing, a notion with clearly negative connotations, denotes conversion to a new religious movement for reasons which are not entirely rational or reasonable.[408] European courts are not at ease about the concept of brainwashing. The main reason why the Italian Constitutional Court abolished in 1981 the criminal offence of *plagio* – translated into English as brainwashing – (Italian Criminal Code, Article 603) is because the provision was too vague and incapable of capturing a[n otherwise equally fluid] real-life phenomenon at the level of precision required of criminal law.[409] As Massimo Introvigne points out, this decision was reached well before fears of brainwashing generated on account of new religious movements became prevalent in Western democracies.[410]

A similar rationale about the vagueness and unsustainability of the concept of brainwashing is also found in Spain. In February 1996, a lower Spanish court said that:

> the term [brainwashing] does not express a scientific concept, but its meanings are many. It has been used at times as a synonym for "mental control", to designate any form of human influence, including hypnosis, psychotherapy, mass media, propaganda, education, behavioural changes, and a constellation of other technical forms for changes in attitude and behaviour.
>
> It is necessary to be very cautious about this concept of "brainwashing", since man is a rational being who builds and structures his thought starting from freely accepted truths, on which he normally bases his values, and therefore those convictions can only be changed by appealing to reason. Consequently the concept of "brainwashing" is meaningless, especially juridically: its "indiscriminate" or "careless" use

---

408. Literature on brainwashing theories is rich and abundant; nonetheless, due to the limitations of this work, it will not be reviewed here.
409. On this, in English, see Introvigne, M., "Brainwashing, Italian-Style: The Rise and Fall of Plagio", at: http://www.cesnur.org/2002/slc/introvigne.htm. The full text of the decision of the Italian Constitutional Court is available in English at: http://www.cesnur.org/2005/brainwashing81.htm.
410. Introvigne, M., "Italy's Surprisingly favourable Environment for Religious Minorities", pp. 75-84, in: Lucas, P. C., and Robbins, T., eds, *New Religious Movements in the 21st Century, Legal Political and Social Challenges in Global Perspective*, Routledge, 2004, p. 78.

may result in a clear meddling in extremely personal rights of the individual, which nobody may impinge.[411]

Despite the reservations of courts, the concept of brainwashing seem to emerge in national legal rules targeting new religious movements. The Czech law on religious associations includes a prohibition on registering sects or cults (Section 5.2.c) which "restrict the personal freedom of individuals, especially through the use of psychological pressure or physical force to create dependence, leading to physical, psychological, or economic harm to persons and their family members, to the disruption of their social relationships, including impairing the psychological development of minors and restricting their right to education, and preventing or inhibiting a minor from receiving health care appropriate to their respective health needs."[412] Consider also the 1997 Russian federal law on the Freedom of Conscience and Religious Associations, Law No. 125-FZ, which provides an elaborate list of grounds for dissolving religious associations (or refusing their re-registration), many of which resemble an anti-sect rationale (Article 14.2). The grounds include:

- infliction of damage established under the law to morals, health of citizens, including the use in connection with their religious activity of narcotic drugs and psychotherapeutic agents, hypnosis, the commission of acts of perversion and other unlawful actions;

- inducement to suicide and refusal for reasons of religion to give medical aid to persons in a state endangering their life and health;

---

411. On quote in Richardson, J. T., "'Brainwashing Claims and Minority Religions Outside the United States: Cultural Diffusion of a Questionable Concept in the Legal Arena", 1996, *Brigham Young University Law Review*, 873, 1996, note 71. The applicant in the case was confined to a mental institution after his mother withdrew him from a Catholic inspiration group (Spanish Society for the Defence of Tradition, Family, and Property) claiming that her son had been programmed and brainwashed. The applicant challenged in court his mother's continuing demand to keep him institutionalised and to declare him mentally incompetent.

412. Act No. 3/2002 Coll. on the Freedom of Religious Expression and the Status of Churches and Religious Societies and Amendments to Certain Acts, 7 January 2002. Available in English at: http://religlaw.org/template.php?id=1752.

- preventing a citizen by using a threat of damage to his life, health, or property, provided there is a real danger of realisation of same, or a threat of violence or by other illegal actions from withdrawing from a religious association;
- forcing members and followers of religious associations and other persons to alienate their property in favour of religious associations.[413]

What makes prohibition of brainwashing appear so compelling in Western democracies? According to Dick Anthony and Thomas Robbins:

> One dimension of the mind control fixation is related to the problematic quality of autonomy in the post-modern world in which an expansion of apparent diversity and choice coexists with both a cultural celebration of individualism and latent anxieties over hidden threats to personal autonomy emanating from mass advertising, state surveillance, new technology, the "iron cage" of bureaucratic rationalism, currents of fanaticism, etc. As James Beckford suggested in *Cult Controversies* (1985), the symbolic and social issues raised by controversies over cults may ultimately be more significant than the movements themselves.[414]

Enquete commissions and sect observatories

In 1982, the European Parliament entrusted the Committee on Youth, Culture, Education, Information and Sport to enquire into the operations of the Unification Church, led by Sun Myung Moon. The rapporteur, Richard Cottrell, submitted a report entitled "The activity of certain religious movements within the European Community" in 1984. In response to the Cottrell report, the Parliamentary Assembly adopted its Recommendation 1178 (1992) on Sects and New Religious Movements. Several national legislatures might be seen as taking inspiration from recommendations of the Parliamentary Assembly of the Council of Europe concerning measures to be taken "in response to the problems raised by some

---

413. As available in English at: http://religlaw.org/template.php?id=1762.
414. Anthony, D. and Robbins, T., "Conversion and 'Brainwashing' in New Religious Movements," pp. 243-297, in Lewis, J. R., eds, *The Oxford Handbook of New Religious Movements*, Oxford, 2003, p. 286.

of the activities of sects or new religious movements".[415] Various European governments and parliaments are known to have undertaken investigations into the activities of religious groups, usually termed as cults or sects which allegedly pose dangers to society.[416] The measures adopted by governments range from parliamentary investigations to the establishment of agencies (so-called sect observatories) and also may include secret service measures.

As seen from its introduction, the decision of the German Constitutional Court quoted above did not arrive in a vacuum.[417] The German federal and state (*Länder*) governments started issuing information booklets about new religious movements in the 1970s and the affected religious groups kept challenging these leaflets in court, eventually leading to the decision of the Constitutional Court, quoted above. In 1996, the German federal parliament also appointed a commission to investigate new religious movements. As Brigitte Schoen points out, the German parliamentary commission was unique in its kind for concluding that these movements did not cause a threat to society.[418] Also, while the decision of the German interior ministry to put Scientology under secret service surveillance is regrettable, all this measure resulted in was further information booklets.

In Belgium,[419] following a lengthy parliamentary investigation, a list of 189 (dangerous and harmless) sects was published, which

---

415. See Recommendation 1178 (1992) on sects and new religious movements adopted by the Parliamentary Assembly on 5 February 1992. For an excellent collection of essays on national legal developments see James Richardson, T., ed., *Regulating Religion: Case Studies From Around the Globe*, Kluwer, 2004.
416. The section does not cover all European enquete commissions and sect observatories in detail.
417. Here, I follow Schoen, B., "New Religions in Germany", pp. 85-95, in: Lucas, P. C. and Robbins, T. eds, *New Religious Movements in the 21st Century, Legal Political and Social Challenges in Global Perspective*, Routlege, 2004, pp. 88-91.
418. The final report is available in English at: www.agpf.de/Bundestag-Enquete-english.pdf.
419. Here, I follow Ferrari, S., "New Religious Movements in Western Europe", *Research and analyses – No. 9*, October 2006, at: http://religion.info/pdf/2006_10_ferrari_nrm.pdf, p. 12. See also Torfs, *Freedom of Religion or Belief in Belgium*, pp. 658 et seq.

was followed by legislation bringing into existence two agencies:[420] an Information and Advisory Centre on Harmful Sectarian Organisations, "mainly devoted to studying, gathering documents, and providing information regarding these groups" and an Administrative Co-ordination Cell for the Fight against Harmful Sectarian Organisations, a body "monitoring the harmful activities of these groups, promoting a policy for their prevention, and coordinating the action of different public authorities". The Belgian Court of Arbitration sustained the law creating the sect observatory in its decision quoted above. Although very few court cases were launched under the Belgian sect monitoring laws, these cases have been seen pending for an extensive period of time.[421] Furthermore, in a separate act, a new division was created in the secret services to monitor terrorism and harmful sects. According to the religious freedom report of the US Department of State in Belgium, "sects were also monitored by local police forces, in particular at the level of judicial districts. Without providing specific detail, the Federal Police identified thirteen sectarian organizations that had potential for threatening public order".[422]

The Belgian solution was in a large part inspired by the measures adopted by subsequent French governments to monitor the activities of new religious movements.[423] Famous among these is the 1996 report of the Gest-Guyard Commission, which contained a list of 172

---

420. Loi du 2 juin 1998 portant création d'un Centre d'information et d'avis sur les organisations sectaires nuisibles et d'une cellule administrative de coordination de la lutte contre les organisations sectaires nuisibles, in *Moniteur belge*, 25 novembre 1998.

421. *Human Rights in the OSCE Region: Europe, Central Asia and North America, Report 2005 (Events of 2004)*, available at: http://www.ihf-hr.org/documents/doc_summary.php?sec_id=3&d_id=4057.

422. Belgium-US State Department, *International Religious Freedom Report, 2006* at: http://www.state.gov/g/drl/rls/irf/2006/71371.htm.
On the operation and decisions of the Belgian sect observatory in English, see Denaux, A., "The Attitude of Belgian Authorities Towards New Religious Movements", 2002, *Brigham Young University Law Review*, 237, 2002. Note that Adelbert Denaux is the president of the Belgian sect observatory (*Centre d'information et d'avis sur les organisations sectaires nuisibles*).

423. Robert, J., "Religious Liberty and French Secularism", 2003, *Brigham Young University Law Review* 637, 2003, pp. 648-649 lists the following characteristics of a cult: small number of adherents, eccentricity, external origin and – most importantly – newness.

dangerous sects, including Jehovah's Witnesses and Scientology. As a follow-up measure, in 1998, another parliamentary commission was established to report on the activities of dangerous sects, issuing the so-called Guyard-Brard Report of 1999. Since 1996, France had a governmental agency specialised on monitoring the sects listed in the parliamentary reports. Since 2002, this task has been performed by the Interministerial Mission of Vigilance and Combat against Sectarian Aberration (*Mission interministérielle de vigilance et de lutte contre les dérives sectaires*) (Miviludes).[424]

According to its founding instrument, the tasks of Miviludes include the duty to promote, while respecting fundamental rights, the co-ordination of preventive and repressive action by the authorities to deal with such behaviour (Article 1.3) and to inform the general public about the risks, and in some cases the dangers, to which it is exposed by sectarian aberrations (Article 1.5). One of Miviludes's controversial attempts to provide information on sects was a guide issued in January 2005 informing public servants about how to identify and combat dangerous sects. In one instance which might be regarded as highly problematic from the freedom of religion perspective, the guide not only informs public servants about Jehovah's Witnesses' conviction in refusing blood transfusion, but also explains in explicit terms that doctors who provide life-saving blood transfusion to patients against their consent are not likely to face negative legal consequences.[425] Reflecting on these developments, Asma Jahangir, the UN Special Rapporteur on freedom of religion or belief warned that the monitoring activities of the French government have led to the undue limitations of rights of religious minorities in France, noting (p. 109) that "the government policy may have contributed to a climate of general suspicion and

---

424. Décret No. 2002-1392 du 28 novembre 2002. The Miviludes report on sectarian activities for the year 2004 is also available in English at: http://www.miviludes.gouv.fr/rubrique.php3?id_rubrique=93. The English translation of the name of the agency was taken from here.
Previously, in 1996, the French government established the Interministerial Observatory on Sects (*l'Observatoire interministériel sur les sectes*), which was subsequently transformed in 1998 into the Interministerial Task Force to Combat Sects (MILS – *Mission interministérielle de lutte contre les sectes*), the task of which was to assist prosecutors in cases involving the criminal activities of sects.
425. *Guide de l'agent public face aux dérives sectaires*, p. 95.

intolerance towards those communities on the list created by the National Assembly in 1996, of movements and groups classified as *sectes*."[426]

Following this report, in the summer of 2006, the French National Assembly established an inquiry commission to investigate the influence of sects on minors, with special emphasis on the psychological and mental impact of sectarian practices on youth (*Commission d'enquête relative à l'influence des mouvements à caractère sectaire et aux conséquences de leurs pratiques sur la santé physique et mentale des mineurs*). The Commission published its 200-page-long report on 29 December 2006.[427] Among many other recommendations, the inquiry commission proposed more express statutory limitations on the right of parents to refuse blood transfusion in their children for reasons of conscience, allowing doctors to proceed with a blood transfusion over parental objection.[428]

In 2001, the French National Assembly passed the About-Picard law, properly entitled as the "Act to reinforce the prevention and repression of sects which infringe human rights and fundamental freedoms". Among other measures, the About-Picard Act allows for the dissolution of "any legal entity, irrespective of its legal form or purpose, which pursues activities with the objective or effect of achieving, maintaining or exploiting the psychological or physical subjection of persons participating in those activities ... where the legal entity itself or its managers, in law or in fact, have been finally convicted of one or more of the offences: 1. The offences of deliberately or unintentionally killing or causing physical or mental harm to others, of endangering others, of infringing personal

---

426. "Civil and political rights, including the question of religious intolerance", Report submitted by Asma Jahangir, Special Rapporteur on freedom of religion or belief, Addendum 2, Mission to France (18-29 September 2005), E/CN.4/2006/5/Add.4, 8 March 2006.
427. Rapport d'enquête relative à l'influence des mouvements à caractère sectaire et aux conséquences de leurs pratiques sur la santé physique et mentale des mineurs No. 3507 déposé le 12 décembre 2006 par M. Philippe Vuilque. The report is available at: http://www.droitdesreligions.net/rddr/commissionenquete.htm.
428. Rapport, ibid., p. 184 (point 18) (The proposed language reads as: *"Dans le cas où ce refus a pour objet une transfusion sanguine, le médecin après avoir informé la personne titulaire de l'autorité parentale ou le tuteur des conséquences de leur choix, procède à la transfusion sanguine."*).

freedoms, of violating human dignity, of interfering with privacy and personal rights, of imperilling minors or the offences against property; 2. The offences of unlawfully practising medicine or pharmacy ...; 3. The offences of misleading advertising, fraud or forgery ... Dissolution proceedings shall be instituted before the Tribunal de Grande Instance at the request of the public prosecutor, acting ex officio, or on an application by any interested party ..." (excerpts from Section 1).[429]

The French act attracted instant criticism from the Council of Europe.[430] The report of the Committee on Legal Affairs and Human Rights prepared by Mr Cevdet Akçali points out (in para 9) that "although it refers explicitly to sectarian movements, the act in fact applies to 'any legal entity, irrespective of its legal form or purpose, which pursues activities with the objective or effect of achieving, maintaining or exploiting the psychological or physical subjection of persons participating in those activities' (...).". So far the law has not been applied to dissolve a religious organisation.[431] When Jehovah's Witnesses challenged the Parliamentary Commission's reports and legislative measures aimed at combating dangerous sects as a violation of their religious freedom under Article 9, the ECtHR found the complaint inadmissible since the law was not

---

429. Quoted from the full, unofficial English translation of the About-Picard law which is provided as an appendix to the report of the Parliamentary Assembly's Committee on Legal Affairs and Human Rights prepared by Mr Cevdet Akçali, Turkey, European Democratic Group (Doc. 9612 of 31 October 2002).

430. Parliamentary Assembly Resolution 1309 (2002) on freedom of religion and religious minorities in France. Text adopted by the Standing Committee, acting on behalf of the Assembly, on 18 November 2002. See Doc. 9612, report of the Committee on Legal Affairs and Human Rights (Rapporteur: Mr Akçali).

431. So far the About-Picard law was applied once, against Arnaud Mussy, the leader or prophet of the Neo-Phare group, a sect or new religious movement. Mussy, who claims to be Christ, announced the immediate arrival of an apocalypse which triggered a sect member to commit suicide, and two others to attempt suicide in 2002. In 2005, the Rennes court of appeal (*cour d'appel de Rennes*) confirmed the conviction for abuse of weakness (*abus de faiblesse*) under the About-Picard law. For an English-language account on the prosecution see Palmer, S. J., "France's About-Picard Law and Neo-Phare: The First Application of *Abus de Faiblesse*", presented at Cesnur 2006 International Conference, 13-16 July 2006, San Diego State University, San Diego, California available online at: http://www.cesnur.org/2006/sd_palmer.htm.

invoked against the Witnesses.[432] Curiously, the ECtHR noted that "it would be inconsistent for the [Witnesses] to rely on the fact that it is not a movement that infringes freedoms and at the same time to claim that it is, at least potentially, a victim of the application that may be made of the Law." This decision duly pinpoints the limits of rights protection on the ECtHR level.

This is not to suggest that legal rules allowing for the dissolution of religious associations are *per se* unacceptable from a human rights perspective. Following the terrorist attacks of 11 September 2001, the German legislature abolished the so-called "religious privilege" which extended the scope of the law governing private associations (*Vereinsgesetz*) to religious organisations, thus making possible the dissolution of religious associations that undermine the liberal and democratic fundamental order in a belligerent and aggressive manner.[433] The German Constitutional Court upheld the law and its application which resulted in a ban on a Muslim organisation called the Caliphate State (*Kalifstaat*) (Decision GER-2003-3-023 a) Germany / b) Federal Constitutional Court / c) Second Chamber of the First Panel / d) 02-10-2003 / e) 1 BvR 536/03 / f) / g) / h) *Europäische Grund-rechtezeitschrift 2003*, pp. 746-749; Codices (German)). In this case, the Constitutional Court upheld the decision of the Federal Administrative Court, which found that the "complainants do not just want to criticise, in an abstract manner, the Federal Republic of Germany's constitutional system while preserving their willingness to act in conformity with the law. They rather intend to assert their own ideas with violent means if necessary."[434]

---

432. *Fédération chrétienne des témoins de Jéhovah de France c. France* (déc.), n. o. 53430/99, 6 novembre 2001, CEDH 2001XI.

433. In 2002, Russia also passed a law banning organisations which engage in extremist activities. See Ferrari, S., "Individual Religious Freedom and National Security in Europe after September 11", 2004, *Brigham Young University Law Review*, 357, 2004, p. 367.

434. "The objective of the *Kalifstaat* was said to be the overthrow of the Turkish secular State and its replacement by a system based on the Shari'a." In Zollner, V., "Liberty Dies by Inches: German Counter-Terrorism Measures and Human Rights", 5(5), *German Law Journal*, 469, 2004, p. 490, available at: http://www.germanlawjournal.com/pdf/Vol05No05/PDF_Vol_05_No_05_469-494_special_issue_Zoeller.pdf.

A major difference between the French About-Picard Act and the German measure is that while the French law targets particular activities loosely associated with sectarian dangers and brainwashing, the German law – although it adversely affected religious communities – does not target religious organisations or activities as such.[435] It is therefore possible to see the German law as an instrument of militant democracy. Sadly, when it comes to protecting Muslim associations from such measures, turning to the ECtHR offers little hope. In *Refah Partisi v. Turkey*, a case involving the dissolution of a Muslim political party in Turkey, the ECtHR said that "a political party whose actions seem to be aimed at introducing sharia in a State party to the Convention can hardly be regarded as an association complying with the democratic ideal that underlies the whole of the Convention."[436] Echoing the opinions of others, Cole Durham submits that there is significant room for doubt concerning the accuracy of the ECtHR's analysis of Islam and Sharia, adding that if the *Refah* decision is understood as an instance of militant democracy jurisprudence, it is distinguishable from religious association cases.[437]

Thus, governmental attempts to monitor religious movement measures may be justified through governments' constitutional duty to protect their citizens from harm, and may even be supported by words of the Parliamentary Assembly of the Council of Europe. While the recommendations stress the need for education about new religious movements, and calls for the establishment of documentation centres to this effect, governmental agencies established to this effect received mixed reviews and seem to fulfil objectives exceeding the aim of educating the polity. This tendency was noted not only by international human rights organisations and NGOs, but also by the Parliamentary Assembly in a more

---

435. The aspect of the German rules which adversely affect foreigners will not be explored here.
436. *Refah Partisi v. Turkey*, Application No. 41340/98, No. 41342/98, No. 41343/98, and No. 41344/98, paragraph 72.
437. Durham, W. C., Jr., "Facilitating Freedom of Religion or Belief through Religious Association Laws", pp. 321-405, in Lindholm, T., Durham, C. W., Jr., Tahzib-Lie, B. G., eds, *Facilitating Freedom of Religion or Belief: A Deskbook*, Martinus Nijhoff, 2004, p. 376.

recent recommendation.[438] Restrictions imposed on the activities of cults, sects or other allegedly dangerous formations of religious communities in several European states call into question the governments' neutrality in matters of religion and belief and have a serious potential in seriously endangering the oldest civic liberty. Unfortunately, however, so far the ECtHR did not appear to be willing to ward off such governmental intrusions.

---

438. Recommendation 1412 (1999) on illegal activities of sects adopted by the Parliamentary Assembly on 22 June 1999.

Select bibliography and suggested further reading

Adhar, R. and Leigh, I., *Religious Freedom in the Liberal State*, Oxford, 2005.

Danchin, P. G. and Cole, E. A., eds, *Protecting the Human Rights of Religious Minorities in Eastern Europe*, Columbia UP, 2002.

Evans, C., *Freedom of Religion under the European Convention on Human Rights*, Oxford UP, 2001.

Evans, M. D., *Religious Liberty and International Law in Europe*, Cambridge UP, 1997.

Ferrari, S., Durham, W. C., Jr., Sewell, E. A., eds, *Law and Religion in Post-Communist Europe*, Peeters, 2003.

Janis, M. W. and Evans, C., eds, *Religion and International Law*, Martinus Nijhoff, 2004.

Lewis, J. R., eds. *The Oxford Handbook of New Religious Movements*, Oxford, 2003.

Lindholm, T., Durham, W. C., Jr., Tahzib-Lie, B. G., eds, *Facilitating Freedom of Religion or Belief: A Deskbook*, Martinus Nijhoff, 2004.

Lucas, P. C., and Robbins, T., eds, *New Religious Movements in the 21st Century, Legal Political and Social Challenges in Global Perspective*, Routledge, 2004.

Massis, T. and Pettiti, C., eds, *La liberté religieuse et la Convention européenne des droits de l'homme*, Bruylant, 2004.

Messner, F., Prélot, P.-H. and Woehrling, J.-M., eds, *Traité de droit français des religions*, Litec, 2003.

Renucci, J.-F., *Article 9 of the European Convention on Human Rights, Freedom of Thought, Conscience and Religion*, Council of Europe, 2005.

Richardson, J. T., ed., *Regulating Religion: Case Studies From Around the Globe*, Kluwer, 2004.

Robbers, G., eds, *State and Church in the European Union*, Nomos, 1996.

Sajó, A. and Avineri, S., eds, *The Law of Religious Identity, Models for Post-Communism*, Kluwer, 1999.

Taylor, P. M., *Freedom of Religion, UN and European Human Rights Law and Practice*, Cambridge UP, 2005.

van der Vyver, J. and Witte, J., Jr., eds, *Religious Human Rights in Global Perspective, Legal Perspectives*, Martinus Nijhoff, 1996.

van der Vyver, J. and Witte, J., Jr., eds, *Religious Human Rights in Global Perspective, Religious Perspectives*, Martinus Nijhoff, 1996.

CODICES : Infobase on Constitutional Case-Law

The database Codices is an electronic publication of the European Commission for Democracy through Law, also known as the Venice Commission (www.Venice.coe.int). Like its printed counterpart, the *Bulletin on constitutional case laws*, Codices regularly reports on the case law of constitutional courts and courts of equivalent jurisdiction – in Europe but also in other parts of the world – together with case law of the European Court of Human Rights and the Court of Justice of the European Communities.

In addition to the more than 5000 summaries of decisions in English and French, Codices contains full texts of the judgments in the original language or in translation, court descriptions, laws on the courts and constitutions. A systematic thesaurus allows for easy access by topic to the summaries, constitutions and laws.

Codices is available via the Internet (www.CODICES.coe.int) and on CD-Rom, which has the advantage of being more user-friendly. The CD-Rom is available from the Council of Europe Publishing.

To Order:
Council of Europe Publishing – Palais de l'Europe
F-67075 Strasbourg Cedex
Tel.: +33 (0)3 88 41 25 81 – Fax: +33 (0)3 88 41 39 10
E-mail: publishing@coe.int – Website: http://book.coe.int

Sales agents for publications of the Council of Europe
Agents de vente des publications du Conseil de l'Europe

BELGIUM/BELGIQUE
La Librairie européenne SA
50, avenue A. Jonnart
B-1200 BRUXELLES 20
Tel.: (32) 2 734 0281
Fax: (32) 2 735 0860
E-mail: info@libeurop.be
http://www.libeurop.be

Jean de Lannoy
202, avenue du Roi
B-1190 BRUXELLES
Tel.: (32) 2 538 4308
Fax: (32) 2 538 0841
E-mail: jean.de.lannoy@euronet.be
http://www.jean-de-lannoy.be

CANADA
Renouf Publishing Company Limited
5369 Canotek Road
OTTAWA, Ontario, K1J 9J3, Canada
Tel.: (1) 613 745 2665
Fax: (1) 613 745 7660
E-mail: order.dept@renoufbooks.com
http://www.renoufbooks.com

CZECH REP./RÉP. TCHÈQUE
Suweco Cz Dovoz Tisku Praha
Ceskomoravska 21
CZ-18021 PRAHA 9
Tel.: (420) 2 660 35 364
Fax: (420) 2 683 30 42
E-mail: import@suweco.cz

DENMARK/DANEMARK
GAD Direct
Fiolstæede 31-33
DK-1171 KOBENHAVN K
Tel.: (45) 33 13 72 33
Fax: (45) 33 12 54 94
E-mail: info@gaddirect.dk

FINLAND/FINLANDE
Akateeminen Kirjakauppa
Keskuskatu 1, PO Box 218
FIN-00381 HELSINKI
Tel.: (358) 9 121 41
Fax: (358) 9 121 4450
E-mail: akatilaus@stockmann.fi
http://www.akatilaus.akateeminen.com

**GERMANY/ALLEMAGNE
AUSTRIA/AUTRICHE**
UNO Verlag
August Bebel Allee 6
D-53175 BONN
Tel.: (49) 2 28 94 90 20
Fax: (49) 2 28 94 90 222
E-mail: bestellung@uno-verlag.de
http://www.uno-verlag.de

GREECE/GRÈCE
Librairie Kauffmann
Mavrokordatou 9
GR-ATHINAI 106 78
Tel.: (30) 1 38 29 283
Fax: (30) 1 38 33 967
E-mail: ord@otenet.gr

HUNGARY/HONGRIE
Euro Info Service
Hungexpo Europa Kozpont ter 1
H-1101 BUDAPEST
Tel.: (361) 264 8270
Fax: (361) 264 8271
E-mail: euroinfo@euroinfo.hu
http://www.euroinfo.hu

ITALY/ITALIE
Libreria Commissionaria Sansoni
Via Duca di Calabria 1/1, CP 552
I-50125 FIRENZE
Tel.: (39) 556 4831
Fax: (39) 556 41257
E-mail: licosa@licosa.com
http://www.licosa.com

NETHERLANDS/PAYS-BAS
De Lindeboom Internationale
Publikaties
PO Box 202, MA de Ruyterstraat 20 A
NL-7480 AE HAAKSBERGEN
Tel.: (31) 53 574 0004
Fax: (31) 53 572 9296
E-mail: lindeboo@worldonline.nl
http://home-1-orldonline.nl/~lindeboo/

NORWAY/NORVÈGE
Akademika A/S Universitetsbokhandel
PO Box 84, Blindern
N-0314 OSLO
Tel.: (47) 22 85 30 30
Fax: (47) 23 12 24 20

POLAND/POLOGNE
Głowna Księgarnia Naukowa
im. B. Prusa
Krakowskie Przedmiescie 7
PL-00-068 WARSZAWA
Tel.: (48) 29 22 66
Fax: (48) 22 26 64 49
E-mail: inter@internews.com.pl
http://www.internews.com.pl

PORTUGAL
Livraria Portugal
Rua do Carmo, 70
P-1200 LISBOA
Tel.: (351) 13 47 49 82
Fax: (351) 13 47 02 64
E-mail: liv.portugal@mail.telepac.pt

SPAIN/ESPAGNE
Mundi-Prensa Libros SA
Castelló 37
E-28001 MADRID
Tel.: (34) 914 36 37 00
Fax: (34) 915 75 39 98
E-mail: libreria@mundiprensa.es
http://www.mundiprensa.com

SWITZERLAND/SUISSE
Adeco – Van Diermen
Chemin du Lacuez 41
CH-1807 BLONAY
Tel.: (41) 21 943 26 73
Fax: (41) 21 943 36 05
E-mail: info@adeco.org

**UNITED KINGDOM/
ROYAUME-UNI**
TSO (formerly HMSO)
51 Nine Elms Lane
GB-LONDON SW8 5DR
Tel.: (44) 207 873 8372
Fax: (44) 207 873 8200
E-mail: customer.services@theso.co.uk
http://www.the-stationery-office.co.uk
http://www.itsofficial.net

**UNITED STATES and CANADA/
ÉTATS-UNIS et CANADA**
Manhattan Publishing Company
468 Albany Post Road, PO Box 850
CROTON-ON-HUDSON,
NY 10520, USA
Tel.: (1) 914 271 5194
Fax: (1) 914 271 5856
E-mail: Info@manhattanpublishing.com
http://www.manhattanpublishing.com

___

FRANCE
La Documentation française
(Diffusion/Vente France entière)
124 rue H. Barbusse
93308 Aubervilliers Cedex
Tel.: (33) 01 40 15 70 00
Fax: (33) 01 40 15 68 00
E-mail: vel@ladocfrancaise.gouv.fr
http://www.ladocfrancaise.gouv.fr

Librairie Kléber (Vente Strasbourg)
Palais de l'Europe
F-67075 Strasbourg Cedex
Fax: (33) 03 88 52 91 21
E-mail: librairie.kleber@coe.int

___

Council of Europe Publishing/Editions du Conseil de l'Europe
F-67075 Strasbourg Cedex
Tel.: (33) 03 88 41 25 81 – Fax: (33) 03 88 41 39 10 – E-mail: publishing@coe.int – Website: http://book.coe.int